Mercedes W113

The Complete Story

OTHER TITLES IN THE CROWOOD AUTOCLASSICS SERIES

Mercedes W113

The Complete Story

Myles Kornblatt

THE CROWOOD PRESS

First published in 2014 by
The Crowood Press Ltd
Ramsbury, Marlborough
Wiltshire SN8 2HR

www.crowood.com

British Library Cataloguing-in-Publication Data
A catalogue record for this book is available from the British Library.

ISBN 978 1 84797 695 6

Typeset and designed by D & N Publishing, Baydon, Wiltshire

Printed and bound in India by Replika Press Pvt. Ltd.

CONTENTS

INTRODUCTION AND ACKNOWLEDGEMENTS

Mercedes-Benz is a car company that has been built out of multiple ideas happening at once. The harmony of these ideas has allowed that company to deliver the world's fastest cars and everyday workhorses under the same three-pointed star. But from their early beginnings as two separate companies at the turn of the twentieth century, to a united industrial giant recovering from the Second World War, the opposing ideas stayed with individual cars. It was only in 1963, with the introduction of the Mercedes 230 SL, that the two paths truly merged.

It has always been hard to define these 'Pagoda' cars. They were modern but elegant; sporting but not blindingly quick; premium but not exotic; safe but not numb; comfortable but not spongy. The W113 model lasted for less than a decade, but its effect will be felt for ever as the car that embodied the entire Mercedes-Benz line in one vehicle.

This book explores the ways in which founding fathers Carl Benz and Gottlieb Daimler built two different companies while both pioneering the automobile. It looks at the merger of two car giants on separate paths, which created one complete car company – a transportation conglomerate that can be recognized equally by its corporate name (first Daimler-Benz, now Daimler), by its company name (Mercedes-Benz), and by various abbreviations (Mercedes, Merc, or Benz).

There were two predecessors to the Pagoda on the market at the same time. One built a cool, speedy image, and the other made owning a roadster comfortable. It was in the Pagoda SL that these two concepts were then brought together.

When the 230 SL came on to the market, it won over both owners and the automotive media on an international scale by being more precise and comfortable than any other sports car available at the time. It was also the right car at the right time for the expansion of Mercedes-Benz in the crucial US market. The successive 250 and 280 SL models would bring more power and features to this line without ruining the design or the well-balanced feel.

This SL would already be prepared for many challenges during its lifetime, but it was not completely immune to the outside world. The carefree era into which the 230 SL was born would rapidly change as the automotive industry was subjected to a tangle of regulations. This book will go beyond the ways in which the Pagoda changed and explore some of the reasons why movements in the USA meant major changes for Mercedes-Benz in Germany.

The W113 is a classic that is kept on the road today both by privateers and by Mercedes. It was a fashion icon when new and today represents a timeless degree of class. Now that the Pagoda SLs are more than half a century old, it is worth taking a closer look at what made them innovative and accommodating, and why they are an everlasting representative of the three-pointed star.

Acknowledgements

Thanks to the National Automotive History Collection at the Detroit Public Library, the Mercedes-Benz Classic Center in Irvine, California and the Revs Institute at The Collier Collection. Archive photos and information are used with the gracious cooperation of Daimler AG. Special thanks to Michael and Patricia Kornblatt.

CHAPTER ONE

ORIGINS – BUILDING THE FASTEST, THE MOST AND THE BEST

Mercedes-Benz was built on the principles of two men who went to great lengths to construct only the best. And, being very early pioneers of automobile technology, they both had moments of self-doubt and an irresistible urge continuously to refine and improve their work. Carl Benz tested his first vehicle only at night so that any hiccups would not gain public attention. Gottlieb Daimler disguised his early innovations so that if there was a problem, others might speculate they were from other inventors.

Carl Benz.

Carl Benz

Carl Benz (who was given the name Karl but preferred to spell it with a 'C') had a tough upbringing. He was born in Karlsruhe, Germany, on 25 November 1844, to a railroad engineer father who died when he was young, and a mother who worked hard to ensure that Benz's poor background would not hinder his education. His mother did not want him to embark on a career in trains, but the mechanical side of the business caught the young man's attention. After attending technical college, he went on to work as a draughtsman for his hometown locomotive works.

By 1871 Benz had started his own machine shop and turned his attention to motor vehicles. While his business fortunes were not the greatest in the beginning, he took a significant step forward with his marriage in 1872. His new wife Bertha Ringer was not only savvy enough to utilize her wedding dowry to rid Carl of an unreliable business partner, but would also provide the catalyst that Benz needed to make progress.

As he built up his fledgling business, Benz decided he needed to create a grand product that the public would find popular. He put his efforts into a developing a two-stroke engine and had spent years trying to get the motor working, without success. Finally, on New Year's Eve 1879, Bertha persuaded him to go over to the machine shop to give the motor another try. The couple saw in the new year with the exhaust note from the two-stroke motor roaring to life for the first time.

On 1 October 1883, Benz created Benz & Cie at his home in Mannheim, and within a year, it was turning a profit as an engine company. Benz was also working on a four-stroke motor that would run in a more refined manner than his two-stroke engine, with which he had now achieved good reliability. Now he finally had the pieces to begin developing a vehicle for the road. Within about a year, Benz had built a 580-lb three-wheeled vehicle with a one-cylinder, four-stroke 954cc motor that produced 0.75bhp.

Benz began testing his new vehicle. On its first run, it did not make it far within the courtyard of the machine shop before needing repair. Subsequent tests would achieve more, but the vehicle still never left the confines of the machine shop's grounds. In January 1886, after more refinements, Benz was granted Patent 37 435 for his first vehicle.

Even with the patent, Benz was still shy about his motor car. All of his testing on the public roads around Mannheim

was performed at night so that any breakdowns would not become fodder for the town gossips. He had built a second car at this point and, although he could get all the way around the city without incident, Benz could not resist tinkering with his invention. Even at these early stages, Carl Benz seemed to be living up to the future slogan of Mercedes-Benz: 'The Best or Nothing.'

By 1886 Bertha Benz was much more convinced about the quality of her husband's car than he was, and she wanted to find a way to prove it. She had a trip scheduled to see her mother 50 miles away in Pforzheim. Rather than take the train as planned, Bertha and the eldest Benz sons awoke before

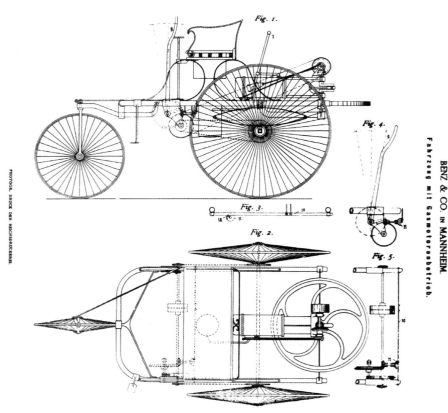

On 29 January 1886 Benz received German patent no. 37 435 on his motorized vehicle.

The Benz family with a
3.5bhp Benz Comfortable
in 1894 (left to right): son
Richard, daughters Thilde
and Ellen, Carl Benz,
daughter Klara and son
Eugen.

Gottlieb Daimler.

dawn. They pushed the vehicle out of the workshop and down the road, until it was far enough away from the house that the motor would not wake Benz, and then they set off. She had at least left him a note explaining where the precious vehicle was!

Bertha was resourceful enough to make a few minor repairs on the road, and she and her sons arrived in Pforzheim by nightfall with no major incident. While this may have been the first case in history of a stolen car, Bertha should certainly get the credit for the first long-distance journey in a Benz. More importantly, she gave her husband the proof he needed in order to feel confident in his motor cars.

Gottlieb Daimler

Gottlieb Daimler was born 50 miles away from and ten years before Carl Benz. The son of a family of Stuttgart bakers, Daimler had a more comfortable upbringing than Benz. Still, it was a series of good mentors and scholarships that gave Gottlieb Daimler the opportunity of a proper education in engineering.

The difference in age meant that Benz and Daimler were not quite at the same stage in their careers as they were both finding their way to the internal combustion engine. The two men did work at the same locomotive firm in Karlsruhe within a few years of each other, but, while Daimler had a managing director position, Benz was still of an age for an entry-level position.

Shortly after completing his engineering education at Stuttgart Polytechnikum in 1860, Daimler would travel Europe learning about the machines of the Industrial Revolution. He returned home to Germany, where he took up a job managing the Bruderhaus Reutlingen near Stuttgart. According to Beverly Rae Kimes, in her book *The Star and the Laurel*, the Bruderhaus was 'part orphanage, part vocational school, part engineering complex … the idea of the Lutheran theologian Gustav Werner and an ingenious religious answer to Marxism'.

Overseeing a workforce of orphans was not going to be a rewarding long-term career for Daimler, but it did introduce him to a star pupil, Wilhelm Maybach. Daimler still believed in a demand for a vehicle that was more personal than the locomotive, and was also sure that steam was not the power of the future. It was a much better fit for him when he joined the Gasmotoren-Fabrik Deutz company as technical manager in 1872. With Maybach in tow as chief designer, Daimler began working on producing internal combustion engines in the company started by Nikolaus Otto, father of the four-stroke engine.

After working for Deutz for a decade, Daimler was out. He wanted to make engines more mobile, and so he and Maybach set to work creating a smaller, lighter four-stroke motor. By 1883 they had a petrol-powered four-stroke that weighed less than 100lb (45.5kg) in an era when the Otto motors weighed as much as 750lb (340kg).

Having developed the engine, Daimler continued to refine it. He installed it on a bicycle, and had his sons run tests of the vehicle, which had effectively become a motorcycle. Daimler and Maybach also installed a new motor in a boat. Just like Benz, Daimler was careful not to let the public in on his testing. Unlike Benz, Daimler would run his boat during the daytime, but he employed decoy electrical terminals near the engine bay so that passengers might assume it was battery powered. Daimler also differed from Benz in that he saw a use for his engine not just in motor cars, but also for all transportation on land and water, and in the air.

Still, a motor vehicle was a priority and something that had not yet been accomplished. By 1886, around the time when Bertha Benz stole her husband's car in order to prove its reliability, Daimler had had a carriage built by W. Wimpff & Sohn. Daimler said it was a birthday present for his wife, but

Daimler's workshop, which he set up at his home in Stuttgart after leaving Deutz.

Daimler's first motorboat on the Neckar River in 1886 (with Daimler and Maybach just right of the motor box).

in fact his plan was to attach his 1.5bhp motor to the structure to create the world's first four-wheeled automobile. Daimler and Benz were now entering the car business at around the same time.

Gottlieb Daimler formed Daimler-Motoren-Gesellschaft (DMG) on 28 November 1890. Once speed laws in Germany were relaxed, DMG would grow to produce some of the most powerful cars of the time. Carl Benz was also doing well; his company would develop into the largest car manufacturer in the world, with production exceeding 600 vehicles at the turn of the century. Between the two men, the vehicles represented significant manufacturing precision and speed.

The era of the motor car had begun, but for one of its pioneers it was the end of his road. Gottlieb Daimler was still part of DMG when he died, on 6 March 1900. There is no record of Carl Benz and Gottlieb Daimler ever formally meeting. After all, at the time of Daimler's death, neither man could have known what the future was for their two companies, and surely neither could have predicted the amazing accomplishments that came with the union.

Duelling Performance and Practicality

Mutton chops and a safari helmet might not seem like a recipe for sales success, but Emil Jellinek was DMG's best customer at the turn of the century. A successful businessman from

Gottlieb Daimler and Wilhelm Maybach's high-speed four-stroke engine with hot-tube ignition.

Emil Jellinek and his daughter Mercedes.

Vienna with an office in Nice, he liked speed and rubbed shoulders with all the right people.

Jellinek was first attracted to the brand when he noticed that Daimler's company built the motors in most of the major race winners. He had purchased a 6bhp belt-driven car in 1897, but found it too slow. He would continue to demand cars with more power. As the factory kept abiding by his requests, Jellinek continued to order more cars that he would sell in France.

As the power ratings kept going up, Jellinek became a more important force on the race circuits. However, people knew him by a different name. During that time racers would often use pseudonyms, and Jellinek decided to borrow his daughter's name, Mercedes.

The racer known as Mercedes became so notable that, when Jellinek placed an order for a 35bhp model, the car would carry his daughter's name rather than the DMG brand. Designed by Maybach, the new car featured such innovations as a pressed-steel frame, gated four-speed transmission, and the honeycomb grille that is now a hallmark. Jellinek was now as much a distributor of Mercedes cars as he was a driver. He knew that the first competition this car really needed to win would be at Nice Week in March. The wealthy citizens of the Riviera would marvel at the creations setting records in their playground, and a victory here would inevitably lead to more sales.

Vehicle assembly at DMG around 1912.

In fact, the Mercedes won all the events during Nice Week. This inspired Jellinek to re-body the car as a four-seater to show the well-heeled of France that the car that dominated their events was not only sporting but also luxurious. The idea proved to be such a good one that it was carried over into new offerings from Mercedes.

The Mercedes became the car to beat or the car to buy. It was so successful that in 1902 DMG registered the trademark and officially renamed the company 'Mercedes'. The next year Jellinek, who was known to have a bit of an ego, obtained permission to call himself Jellinek-Mercedes, saying: 'This is probably the first time that a father has taken his daughter's name.'

Meanwhile, Carl Benz was falling a little behind the times. He believed in high-quality, low-powered cars. As executives within his company were going around him to have higher-performance models developed, Benz realized that it was time to step away. On 24 January 1903, Benz announced his retirement from the board of directors and took a seat on the Supervisory Board. Now with both patriarchs out of the day-to-day operations, the newly christened Mercedes and the Benz automobile companies would spend the next decade building international empires based on swiftness and substance.

The outbreak of the First World War put the brakes on the need for speed, and both Benz and DMG went into aircraft production. In 1916 DMG built a new factory in Sindelfingen, outside Stuttgart, to increase aircraft production. The factory would become significant in the future, but by the time peace was declared, in 1919, it was just dead weight. In fact, both Benz and DMG found themselves in a bad way after the war. The collapse of the German economy and the temporary loss of its international dealer network had Benz and DMG seriously entertain the idea of merging companies only a few months after the signing of the peace treaties. However, the two sides could not quite agree to terms, and the companies stayed independent … for the time being.

Instead of joining forces, the companies dug deeper into technical advances. In what seemed to fit with the early days, when their respective founders were in charge, Mercedes went for power while Benz went for practicality. DMG would advance its horsepower with the development of the supercharger, and Benz decided that diesel motors could provide a helpful alternative in transportation.

While the companies had retreated into their workshops, private drivers had begun to take their cars off to the tracks again. In 1921 Count Louis Zborowski began mixing modified Mercedes chassis with aircraft engines to run the Easter Meeting at the Brooklands track in England. This car was nicknamed 'Chitty Bang Bang' for the raucous noise produced by the aero engine. Count Zborowski's first car, Chitty I, used a

Benz did have racing credential such as the 1909 Blitzen-Benz.

Mercedes engine, but Chitty II, in common with another creation by the British firm C.H. Crowe & Company, mixed the Mercedes chassis and a Benz aero engine. While these men had no idea of the future, they were creating the first unofficial Mercedes-Benz racing cars. It would not be long before the name became a bit more official.

Both companies were trying to get back to the normal business of producing winning racing cars and luxury passenger cars in the early 1920s. Unfortunately, the runaway German economy was making matters very difficult. A customer named Jakob Schapiro was draining the company resources by ordering chassis for his coach-building business on credit, and using the float time and massive inflation to pay Benz very little for their product. At the same time as he was weakening the company, Schapiro was also buying up Benz stock.

With the company about to be taken over, Benz needed a strong ally, and it was Emil Georg von Stauss who now took an interest. Using his position with Deutsche Bank and on the DMG board, he began to bring the two car companies closer. In May 1924, DMG and Benz signed an 'Agreement of Mutual Interest', which pooled parts of the dealer network as well as refining the automotive product to be more complementary.

This was not initially an easy pairing. In the two decades after Carl Benz's departure from being hands-on with Benz & Cie, the peacetime agenda was focused on competing with DMG. Benz engines got larger, and while they kept producing more entry-level cars, a fellow German was pushing Mercedes off the racetrack. Overlap would be addressed in the interest of survival, and on 28 June 1926, Daimler-Benz AG was registered. The cars with the three-pointed star and the cars with the laurel merged to all be the star and the laurel of Mercedes-Benz.

With financial matters settled, and the economy on the mend, Mercedes-Benz got down to the business of building cars for the track and the road. The new products carried the tradition of covering a very wide market. For example, the only feature shared by the Mercedes-Benz Stuttgart 200 saloon and the Mercedes-Benz SSK was a six-cylinder engine. The 200 Stuttgart had a dependable and prudent image, and its

The three-pointed star and the laurel were combined for the new Mercedes-Benz symbol.

The Mercedes SSK and two premium saloons carrying Maybach's name on display at Auto & Technik Museum Sinsheim, Germany.

2.0-litre frugal engine made it the favourite of Germany's taxi drivers. The 1928 SSK ('SS' for Super Sport, and 'K' for *kurtz* or 'short') – Ferdinand Porsche's swan-song with the company – was a shorter and lighter version of the already competitive SS car. Its 7.1-litre supercharged motor produced 200bhp at its introduction in 1928 but was up to 250bhp when the last of the 31 total production was completed in 1932.

The only car rarer than the SSK was the SSKL ('L' for 'light'), on which drilling holes in everything from the chassis to the brake pedal had saved 250lb (114kg). Only seven of these 300bhp race track dominators were made, and none is known to survive. This would be the first time a Mercedes-Benz would carry both 'Sport' and 'Light' in its name but certainly not the last.

By the time America's Great Depression reached Germany, the Mercedes-Benz line-up was at its broadest ever. For the wealthiest of the world, Mercedes had introduced the Type 770. The 7.7-litre machine topped out with a supercharger and convertible body at RM 47,500. At the other end of the spectrum was the most economical car Mercedes-Benz had introduced to date. The new Type 170 undercut the Stuttgart saloon by over 25 per cent at RM 4,400. Including such features as independent swing axles for the front and rear suspension, the little 1.7-litre car was considered quite good value. By 1932, after a full year of production, Mercedes had produced 4,481 Type 170 models, which was more than the total number of all passenger car models produced by the company in the previous year.

Manfred von Brauchitsch with a streamlined Mercedes-Benz SSKL at the Avus race at Berlin.

A 1928 Mercedes-Benz 680 S with a body by the famed French firm Saoutchik, winning the 2012 Pebble Beach Concours d'Elégance.

RUDOLF UHLENHAUT

A less than stellar Grand Prix race season in 1936 led to a radical decision for Mercedes racing, with the creation of a new division specifically to focus on getting the tri-star back in the winner's circle. It would prove to be one of the company's most fruitful moves.

Daimler-Benz's first racing department was put in the hands of 30-year-old Rudolf Uhlenhaut, a young engineer with the driving skills of a professional racer. He took the 1936 GP cars to the Nürburgring and personally wore both vehicles out. Uhlenhaut realized that the chassis and suspension felt much like those of the company's passenger cars, so he immediately set about developing a bespoke vehicle for the track. The result was the W127 Silver Arrow, in which Rudolf Caracciola would win the 1937 European Championship Grand Prix.

The Third Reich offered some partial racing subsidies to both Mercedes and Auto Union, but it had high expectations of nothing but success. This sparked an intra-country rivalry between the tri-star and the four rings, and in the end led to the creation of some of the most radical racing vehicles to date. Under the guidance of Rudolf Uhlenhaut, the racing department, and its ace driver Rudolf Caracciola, went chasing speed records. In January 1938 Mercedes was responsible for a streamlined machine that raised the top speed bar to 268mph (nearly 429km/h).

After the end of the Second World War, Uhlenhaut was eager to get back to racing. In the first half of the 1950s, he would develop the 300 SL (W194), the post-war Silver Arrows (W196), and the 300 SLR (W196 S). And even after the curtain had fallen on the racing department, Uhlenhaut still had speed in his heart – he took a 300 SLR chassis and gave it a touring car gullwing body to create his own personal race car.

Uhlenhaut was also made Head of Passenger Car Research at Daimler-Benz in the early 1950s. Not only were the 300 SL and 190 SL road cars produced during his tenure, but it also carried him into the development of the W113 Pagoda SL, as well as its successor. Uhlenhaut retired in 1972, leaving the legacy of the iconic W116 S-Class as his last creation.

Rudolf Uhlenhaut with the 300 SL overlooking Stuttgart in 1953.

1937 540 K Spezial Roadster at a 2011 auction.

Although Germany would climb out of the economic turmoil under a dark cloud, there was new vigour in the automotive industry, which benefited from a relaxation on taxes. Mercedes arguably hit its high watermark in passenger cars in 1936 with the 540 K – 2.5 tons of rolling sculpture. With 180bhp on tap this was also the fastest non-racing production car at the time, with a top speed above 105mph (168km/h)

Mercedes had not, however, completely abandoned its practicality at this time. In the same year, 1936, the company also introduced the 260 D, the first diesel engine production car. Where the 540 K was a display of opulence, the 260 D represented a continuation of the tradition of sturdy economy. Both were part of the same Mercedes-Benz catalogue.

Daimler-Benz was also responsible for producing the 30 prototype vehicles that would eventually become the Volkswagen Beetle. Hitler had started building a brand-new factory for these little cars, but it was Mercedes that was the only company to have a significant pre-production run before the outbreak of the Second World War.

CHAPTER TWO

THE BIRTH OF THE SL

Mercedes-Benz factories were an important target during the Second World War, and every one of the company's plants was in need of repair at the end of the conflict. In a time when it was hard to come by food let alone steel, getting production started up again was a slow process. In 1946, Mercedes-Benz was able to produce only 214 of its 170V saloon, which had been designed before the war. However, once the German Economic Miracle was in full swing, recovery came at a rapid pace; by 1950, production of the 170V saloon had grown to 11,876. Even more importantly, there were new models on the horizon, including the 220 saloon and its upmarket sibling the 300 series.

While passenger cars were a priority, some at Mercedes-Benz were immediately ready to return to the racetrack. Rudolf Uhlenhaut was still head of the racing department, and he was already ready to compete when production re-started in 1946. Although he had designs in hand, a lack of resources and manpower meant, however, that he would have to wait a few years before he could develop a new racing programme.

Wind-tunnel measurements with the W194 and its close mechanical sibling, the 300 S (W188).

With the launch in 1951 of the 300 series, Mercedes went back to its old business of having one line of cars for the masses, alongside some more exclusive models. With a new luxury model and six-cylinder engine in production, the Daimler-Benz board gave its approval to a new motorsport plan. The ultimate goal was to return to the world of Formula 1 Grand Prix racing in time for the 1954 rule changes. Included in this grand design was a sports-car programme utilizing many parts already in production so that Mercedes could re-establish its name in competition before the F1 car was ready.

SL Born for the Track

The starting point for the new sports car would be the new 300 S, a higher-performance cabriolet model that took the 3.0-litre straight six from 115bhp to 150bhp. Uhlenhaut's team worked on the intake and exhaust to raise the motor (now designated M 194) to 170bhp. This was shy of the 200bhp that Uhlenhaut thought Mercedes-Benz needed to be competitive, but he had a few tricks up his sleeve to keep his new cars viable.

The W194, as it was known internally at Mercedes, utilized a new form of chassis construction known as a spaceframe. Borrowing a technique from the aviation industry, rather than building a car on a ladder chassis, the car was held together by a series of small steel tubes. Uhlenhaut and his

ABOVE RIGHT: **Models for the spaceframe, made from welding wire, were used to test torsional rigidity.**

Front axle of W194 chassis #2 with perforations made for weight reduction.

men built scale models in order to identify the points at which there would be the largest stress loads, to determine where and how the tubing would be welded together to make a complete car. The result was a 94.5in wheelbase chassis that came in at 110lb (50kg).

The body would utilize lightweight aluminium in a few unique ways. First, most of the sports cars competing at the time were open roadsters, which benefited from the weight savings gained by not having a metal roof fitted on the car. Instead, Uhlenhaut chose to build his car as a closed coupé because he believed the lower drag coefficient would give his racers an advantage.

To keep the car as low as possible, the tall saloon-based engine was tilted 50 degrees to the right so that the car could retain a low bonnet line. This also necessitated a dry-sump lubrication system so that the tilted engine always had oil. A four-speed manual gearbox was then added.

Once the body was chosen, there was the new problem of how to get the driver in and out of the car. Regulations at the time demanded that every vehicle have a 16 x 8in (40 x 20cm) set of doors, and cutting that kind of hole out of a spaceframe chassis could cripple it. Uhlenhaut came up with a brilliant solution that started the door at the window and had it cut upwards, where it was hinged near the centre of the roof. The steering wheel was also removable to make it easier for drivers getting into and out of this new door arrangement.

The suspension was another piece that came from the 300 series parts bin. Up front were unequal-length upper and lower wishbones. Also included were coil springs, telescopic dampers, and an anti-roll bar. In the rear was an independent dual-joint swing-axle set-up that utilized coil springs and telescopic dampers. The rear torsion bars needed for the heavy saloon were discarded for the light

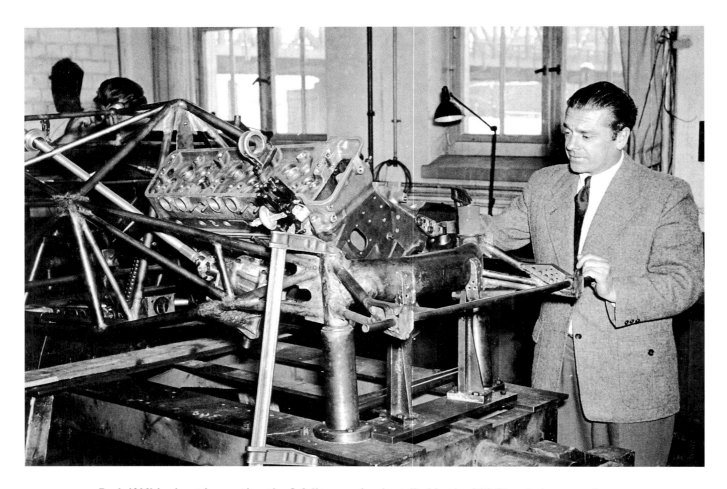

Rudolf Uhlenhaut inspecting the 3.0-litre engine installed in the 300 SL tubular spaceframe.

Mercedes-Benz 300 SL (W194) chassis number 0001.

racing car. Al-fin drums on all four wheels provided the stopping power. Some refinement was added to the suspension because Uhlenhaut believed that driver comfort would help him to combat fatigue and therefore improve his performance.

The sleek coupé tipped the scales at 2,340lb (1,064kg). This may not seem like the most svelte car out there – the more powerful Jaguar C-Type had an advantage of about 250lb (114kg) – but one-fourth of the racer's weight came from the production spec engine. While plenty more mass could have been shed if Uhlenhaut had been able to develop a new engine for the car, it was still a 1,050lb (477kg) saving over the 300 S. The Sport Leicht ('sports light'), or SL, was born.

Taking the W194 Racing

Mercedes racing team manager Alfred Neubauer had agreed with Uhlenhaut's original wishes to have 200bhp in the new race car now known as the 300 SL. He knew the Jaguars and Ferraris would weigh less than his cars, and so he wanted the strongest engine possible. Neubauer believed that more power, a five-speed transmission, larger tyres, and larger brakes were all necessary to make the 300 SL competitive. Unfortunately, by 1952, Mercedes was already stretched with other production and development programmes, including plans for its return to Grand Prix racing, so the 300 SL would have to hit the track as it was.

Even with Neubauer's announced shortcomings, the 300 SL was built to mark Mercedes-Benz's triumphant return to racing. Neubauer was competitive, and was prepared to go as far as he could in order to make these cars into winners. He wanted his drivers to become familiar with the lightweight and aerodynamic advantages of the 300 SL and to know how to utilize them. When the 1952 Mille Miglia endurance race was chosen for the 300 SL's debut, Mercedes spent 2 months having the cars and drivers make between 10 and 16 practice runs of the 1,000-mile (1,600-km) Italian course. According to the *Daily Press*, the fuel costs alone represented an outlay of £2,000.

Uhlenhaut knew he had a unique car, possibly too unique. When the W194 300 SLs showed up for the actual Mille Miglia race, there were three competitors and one spare car. Curiously, this standby's doors were larger than those of the other cars, because its opening dipped below the window line and into the side. With the doors open above the roof, this extension added a new curve in the silhouette that made onlookers compare it to a gull in flight. It soon acquired its nickname of 'gullwing'. More important than its appearance was the fact that the reserve car was almost the only one that would have been allowed to compete in the race. The openings on the 300 SL had originally been deemed illegal by the Italian race authorities. It was only following the intervention of Conte Aymo Maggi, creator of the race, that it was given official authorization to take part.

The three cars were piloted by an all-German team of drivers: Karl Kling, Herman Lang and Rudolf Caracciola. The

ALFRED NEUBAUER

Alfred Neubauer.

Alfred Neubauer did not have a spectacular career as a race driver, but he was destined to change the sport for ever. He had come to DMG with Ferdinand Porsche in 1923 to work in the test centre. By the time Daimler and Benz were beginning to merge, Neubauer was on his way out of the driver's seat. His mind was still on racing, however, as he turned his attention to solving problems on the track.

Mercedes had won the first German Grand Prix, held at the AVUS track in July 1926, but driver Rudi Caracciola was just happy that he had successfully completed the gruelling and rain-soaked race. Caracciola was unaware that he had delivered his first major victory for Mercedes. Neubauer was all too familiar with the isolation that happens on a race track. These were the days before radio communications, and the only time a driver got information was when he pulled off the track. The fact that Caracciola had won by a few minutes, but had been completely unaware of his position in the race, had Neubauer searching for a better answer. He officially retired from racing and became a race director.

By the end of the year Neubauer had created signal boards and special flags to provide information to the drivers on the track. The drivers could communicate with the pits by using a sign language that allowed them to flash specific questions to their crew, including number of laps and the position of other cars on the circuit. Neubauer became a model of efficiency, and his drivers became better competitors for it.

Neubauer led Mercedes in the 1934–39 era, during which the Silver Arrows captured many Grand Prix victories and land-speed records. He would return to the racing department after the Second World War to oversee the 300 SLs to success in 1952. The string of wins would continue with the return to GP racing in 1954 and the 300 SLR in 1955. The racing programme halted at the end of 1955, and Neubauer stayed with Mercedes until 1962.

51-year-old Caracciola was by far the veteran of the group, and possibly the most intriguing driver for the crowd, as one who had won the 1931 Mille Miglia in a Mercedes SSKL – the first car and driver from outside Italy to win the event. Mercedes' main competitors were the brand-new 230bhp Ferrari 225 S Vignale driven by Giovani Bracco and Stirling

Moss' Jaguar C-Type with Dunlop disc brakes. Both cars presented stiff competition, running faster and stopping sooner than the 300 SL.

Kling made sure to drive his Mercedes hard. As Bracco's Ferrari developed tyre problems, Kling took an early lead, averaging around 93mph (149km/h) in the wet conditions.

W194s showing the initial door design (far) and improved 'gullwing' (near).

Racing in Bern on 18 May 1952, with each car fully painted a different colour.

Moss's Jaguar retired with a ruptured fuel tank. He had his sights on third place when the Jag dropped out, which helped Caracciola move up in the race standings. However, not all Mercedes drivers were fortunate: Lang's journey ended during a run-in with a stone marker.

Meanwhile, at the front of the pack, Bracco was battling back from his earlier de ay. His Ferrari would regain the top spot fittingly on the way to Modena, but his tyres soon gave him trouble once again, clearing the way for Kling to retake the lead. Towards the end, fortunes switched again, with the Mercedes developing brake trouble before the finish line, allowing Bracco to take the chequered flag.

Although it was not a win for Mercedes, it was a good showing for the 300 SL's first major outing. Kling's time of 12 hours 14 minutes 17 seconds was beaten into second place by only 4 minutes 35 seconds. And, despite some plug trouble, Caracciola was still able to take fourth, behind Luigi Fagioli's Lancia Aurelia.

Later that spring Kling, Lang and Caracciola took to the wheel of the 300 SL once again, driving the same cars at Berne. This time there was also a fourth entry as Mercedes had Fritz Riess drive the long-door back-up car in the Swiss race. Where the 300 SLs had raced strictly in German sliver for the Mille Miglia, this time the cars were painted green for Kling, blue for Lang, and red for Caracciola. The car that Riess was driving was already extremely distinctive and remained in bare aluminium.

As Berne was more of a shakedown for Le Mans than a full competition, Mercedes had light opposition. It was even less of a challenge once the only factory Ferrari entry had retired early. Mercedes took a 1-2-3 victory with Kling, Lang and Riess (respectively), but all was not perfect. The rear brake locked on Caracciola's 300 SL causing a crash that would give him a broken leg and end the celebrated Mercedes-Benz driver's career.

Le Mans

Mercedes sent three competitors and two spares to France for the 1952 Le Mans 24-hour race. The three in the race were new 300 SLs built with the larger door arrangement so that Mercedes would not run into any more trouble with regulations at a major event. Driving partners were Kling and Hans Klenk (Kling's co-driver during the Mille Miglia), Lang and Riess, and Theo Helfrich and Helmut Nidermayr, who were new to the team after Caracciola's retirement. Their cars would once again sport the traditional German silver livery, but a similar colour scheme to that used in Berne was painted around the grille in order to identify the drivers.

This was a nervous race for Mercedes. Neubauer was worried about the 300 SL's lack of power and he did not have high expectations. The threat that had been presented by Ferrari and Jaguar at the Mille Miglia was once again in full effect. In addition, Mercedes suffered a further disadvantage because of

Running start for the 1952 24 Hours of Le Mans.

the traditional Le Mans standing start: after they had entered through the gullwing doors, the Mercedes drivers needed to take an extra few seconds to refit their steering wheels.

As Neubauer had feared, the lower-powered Mercedes cars struggled to keep up on the track, but legendary Mercedes build quality would prove to be a great advantage. Before dawn on Sunday, overheating had taken out all of the of the Jaguar C-Types and most of the feared Ferraris, while Kling's car was the only Mercedes to fail.

Kling's electrical problems were especially unfortunate because he was the lead 300 SL in the race at the time, with the other two cars holding on to fifth and seventh place. As the more powerful, but less reliable, cars ahead of Lang/Riess and Helfrich/Nidermayr continued to retire, they were able to move up into second and third.

As the race went into its final afternoon, Frenchman Pierre Levegh was in the lead. The engine in his Talbot-Lago T26 GS

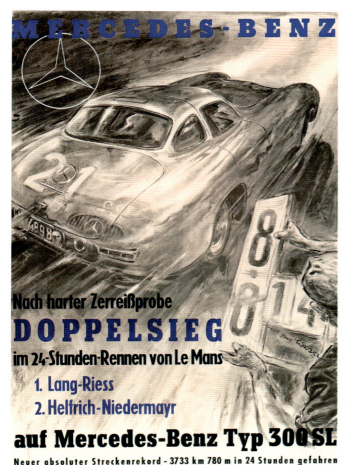

Poster celebrating the 300 SL's victory at Le Mans.

had 50 per cent more capacity than the 300 SL, so it looked very likely that he would be able to deliver a victory to his home crowd. Once again, however, the issue of reliability played a part. Levegh was exhausted from driving the 24-hour race all on his own, while Neubauer had stuck to his strategy of keeping drivers rested and unstressed. With just 72 minutes left in the race, Levegh is believed to have over-revved his engine in error, causing a connecting rod to break. This cleared the way for Lang and Riess to take the top honours, with Helfrich and Nidermayr not far behind in second place.

Finishing the Season and the W194's Career

While a 1-2 victory at Le Mans is an internationally celebrated feat, Mercedes was back later that summer in full force at the support race for the German Grand Prix. Mercedes did not have an entry in the main GP race but still wanted to put on a good show for the home crowd. Six cars were entered in the event – two coupés and four roadsters – all with the identifying colour accent moved from the grille to around the headlights.

One advantage of the 300 SLs had been their aerodynamic coupé design. This was going to be less of a benefit at the Nürburgring because it was a shorter course. With less of a need for a clean slipstream, lightness would be the key in the race. The decision was made to try a few W194 roadsters for the first time. Mercedes saved 220lb (100kg) by cutting the tops off of a few 300 SL coupés. Converting these cars into roadsters was not too difficult, as the rigid spaceframe could provide stiffness with or without an alloy top. Another variation was some 300 SLs were adapted for a narrower wheelbase. Lang won the race in a roadster with his teammates not too far behind. Mercedes had a 1-2-3-4 victory at this home event.

There were other variations of the 300 SL, with shorter wheelbases and supercharged engines, but it was an original wheelbase roadster that won the race, with Lang at the wheel. Other W194s were not far behind and Mercedes had a 1-2-3-4 victory at this home event.

With reliability being one of the most significant factors in the 300 SL's success, Mercedes decided to accept an invitation to the notoriously rough Carrera Panamericana. Four 300 SLs were sent across the Atlantic for the 2,000-mile (3,200-km) race across Mexico. Kling and Klenk were teamed up once again and Lang was now partnered with Erwin Grupp. This was the race in which American John Fitch began his career with Mercedes, partnering Eugen Geiger in the sole roadster competitor. (The last car at this race was a spare roadster.)

Winning drew crowds as the 300 SL took centre stage at the 1953 International Motor Show in Frankfurt.

Hermann Lang on his way to winning at the Nürburgring on 3 August 1952.

There was no 3-litre class at this race so the Mercedes was free bored to a final capacity of 3103cc, which yielded 177bhp. It was still short of the desired 200bhp, but the 300 SLs proved none the less to be some of the best performers ever seen at this young race. Although the team suffered collisions with all sorts of obstacles, from a dog to a buzzard, Kling took first and Lang earned second place in the race. Fitch was disqualified during a pitting. Another set of 1-2 finishes was not only impressive, but the Carrera Panamericana would also mark a crucial step in the transformation of the Mercedes SLs into the cars of today.

ABOVE: **The 1952 Carrera Panamericana-winning 300 SL (complete with buzzard protection), returning to the track in 2010.**

RIGHT: **Promotion piece touting the 300 SL's victories in 1952.**

SPORT-WAGEN
MERCEDES-BENZ 300 SL
ERFOLGE 1952
MILLE-MIGLIA BRESCIA
2. 4. PREIS
GROSSER PREIS DER SCHWEIZ
(BERN) 1. 2. 3. PREIS
24 STUNDEN-RENNEN VON
LE MANS 1. 2. PREIS
JUBILÄUMSPREIS VOM
NÜRBURGRING 1.2.3.4. PREIS
III. CARRERA PANAMERICANA
MEXICO 1. 2. PREIS

CHAPTER THREE

SLs HIT THE ROAD

Hobel is compared to a 1952 300 SL racer.

Utilizing what were once spark-plug holes, the W198 had the world's first four-stroke engine with fuel injection.

Uhlenhaut was ready to return to the track for 1953. The 300 SL had an impressive first year on the circuit, but the Mercedes racing designer wanted to address its shortcomings. He took W194 chassis #11 and began to make improvements almost everywhere.

While the production-based straight-six engine remained, the spark plug holes were now the mounting points for fuel injection – the Bosch unit was a first for petrol-powered Mercedes cars. The plugs were relocated to the top of a revised head that now also included larger valves. The compression ratio was raised from 8:1 to 8.6:1, and the final result gave Uhlenhaut the motor he always wanted. This engine surpassed the 200bhp he desired for the 1952 season; the final output of 214bhp represented a 26 per cent gain over the original 300 SL engine.

The test car was known as 'Hobel' and sported a number of exterior improvements. The body became more efficient, with a wider opening at the front to take in more cool air,

Hobel making an appearance on the lawn at the 2012 Pebble Beach Concours d'Elégance.

and vents at the back of the engine bay to expel hot air more quickly. The bonnet was lowered to the point at which a bulge needed to be placed on the right side for the sideways engine to clear (the bulge on the left was just for vanity). At the back there were vents for the brakes and a smoother sculpted rear end.

Even with all these improvements, the car was still not seen as the perfect racer. It was still less powerful than the previous year's Ferrari, and there was no doubt that Enzo would be aiming directly at Mercedes for the 1953 season. The 300 SL finished 1952 with an impressive list of wins, made possible only by Mercedes-Benz's reliability mixed with a little bit of luck. The 300 SL had accomplished its goal of re-establishing Mercedes on the racing scene, but it looked unlikely to repeat its successes.

Daimler-Benz's ultimate objective was to return to Grand Prix racing in 1954. Rather than invest more resources for the W194, the decision was made to sit out the 1953 season and focus on the upcoming W196 race car. This would mean that Hobel would never make it to the track, but its story did not end there.

Coming to America

Max Hoffman became the USA distributor for Mercedes-Benz in 1952 just as the 300 SLs were making a splash in Europe at Le Mans, and later on Hoffman's home continent at the Carrera Panamericana. He could sell the luxury cars, but the European racing machines were what the Americans were really after. Hoffman wanted a road-going 300 SL for his showroom in New York, but at first Mercedes was not too keen on the idea. According to legend, Hoffman managed to convince them to go ahead by placing an order for between 500 and 1,000 road-legal 300 SLs.

Mercedes decided to resurrect the ideas seen in Hobel to create the first road-going 300 SL – a car that would be known as W198. The world got its first peek at this machine when it premiered in Hoffman's home city at the 1954 New York International Auto Show.

Possibly the best Hobel upgrade to make it into the production car was the 214bhp fuel-injected engine. The lines of the consumer car were based on the Hobel design but made more elegant. The new 300 SL had more curves on the front end, and

Mercedes-Benz 300 SL at the 1954 New York International Motor Sports Show.

MAXIMILIAN HOFFMAN

Max Hoffman.

Max Hoffman was responsible for giving the United States a taste of Europe. In the 1930s he gave up auto racing to become a dealer for the French Amilcar in his homeland of Austria. He would end that decade with a move to Paris and eventually New York as the Second World War came closer. Deciding to stay in America after the conflict, he re-established his dealership in 1947, placing just one car, a four-passenger Delahaye coupé, in his new Manhattan showroom.

The showroom soon filled up as Hoffman spotted a good marketing opportunity. US soldiers were returning from Europe and bringing back sports cars that they could not get at home. Hoffman became the US importer for English roadster brands such as Jowett, Healey and Allard, and he is credited with establishing Jaguar's success on the American market. He also went to mainland Europe to bring back brands such as Alfa-Romeo, Simca and Lancia, but he always had a soft spot for vehicles produced close to his homeland, such as Porsche, BMW and Mercedes-Benz. As the sole distributor of these brands for half or all of the country, Hoffman did not just sell through his own New York showroom, but was also the wholesale contact for many import car dealerships across the USA.

Hoffman's business began to come unstuck with his distribution of Volkswagens. VW's road to export profits would come from large volume, but Hoffman preferred to use the little Beetle as part of an incentive scheme. If a dealer asked him for a popular sports car he would apparently offer it only on the condition that they take a few VWs as well. While Hoffman was representing Volkswagen, any showroom in the USA displaying popular cars from brands such as Porsche, Jaguar and Mercedes, might also have had a few unwanted VWs on the premises. Volkswagen decided to end their agreement with Hoffman. They were not the only manufacturer to do so; many of the bigger brands would eventually leave the Hoffman stable, but he was not necessarily always the loser. For example, his relationship with Mercedes caused him to lose his contract with rival Jaguar, but the buyout became quite lucrative as it included a royalty for each car sold in Hoffman's former territory for many years to come.

Hoffman's reputation lay in finding the right marques to introduce to the USA. As a dealer with good distribution contacts in America, he would start the brands off well, but he was inefficient in handling large volumes. A buyout was often his reward for growing the brand to a size that would allow the the company to establish its own subsidiary. It was a winning situation for both side: Hoffman would grow richer, and the foreign car companies would benefit from a cultivated market. Mercedes was one of the quickest at this, outgrowing Hoffman within 7 years of the Second World War.

Besides Mercedes vehicles, Hoffman helped distribute other German imports to dealers throughout the USA, including Porsche and Volkswagen (briefly).

the front-hinged bonnet lid was set back from the edge of the grille. Designers were using chrome all over other cars of this era, but on the 300 SL its use was more restrained, on areas such as the wheels, grille, headlight surround and bumpers. The final touch was the eyebrow arches over the wheels, which Mercedes claimed had aerodynamic properties. Regardless of

function, they gave the new road car a visual link to the W196 racer, while adding an air of elegance.

Mercedes' policy of keeping its race drivers comfortable meant that less work was required in adapting the interior of the 300 SL for street use. The driver and passenger had enough interior space in the 94.5in wheelbase in the race

ABOVE AND ABOVE RIGHT: **The road-going 300 SL is an obvious descendent from the W194.**

The road-going 300 SL's interior was afforded more luxuries than the racer.

car that it was able to carry over into the passenger vehicle. The race-spec driver buckets were swapped for wider, more comfortable units, but they still came upholstered in Mercedes-Benz Racing's traditional tartan material as standard (leather optional). The dash panel had to carry more items than the 300 SL ever did in its racing days. A number of features, from heating/ventilation levers to a passenger-side horn button, were added to the road-ready version.

Boot space was never given much consideration in Hobel, which meant rear storage was limited in the production car. On the racer, it was necessary to accommodate only the fuel tank and the spare wheel, and, although the road-going gullwing was given a slightly longer tail end, its boot did not hold much more. Mercedes knew the 300 SL would be performing some grand touring duty in the hands of pedestrian owners, so they made fitted luggage available that could be strapped into the shelf behind the occupants.

One particular problem from the racing days demanded a creative solution. Mercedes could not expect its retail customers to remove the steering wheel every time they wanted to climb into the driver's seat, as the race-car drivers had had to do. The innovative solution involved the wheel being hinged at its bottom. As the driver got into the car, he could pull a lever that allowed the steering wheel to angle downwards,

giving his legs enough room. Once he was settled into his seat, he could tilt the wheel back upwards and begin his journey.

The famous gullwing doors also required some adjustments if they were to be suitable for civilian life. The handles on the W194 racers had a simple lever at the base of the window outside and a sliding bolt inside to keep the door in place. This would hardly provide security for a car parked in the middle of a city so a proper mechanism had to be fitted. On the car presented at the New York International Motor Sports Show the exterior door handle was recessed into the bodywork, but on all production cars it stayed flush with the car body until the button was pressed to release the handle. Also, the simple props used to hold up the racer doors were replaced with gas struts for the road cars.

Because of the shape of the door, there was no way to build wind-down windows into the frame. The use of window ports was not much of a problem for the W194 racer but, unfortunately for Mercedes-Benz, this would hardly be suitable for a road car. The car at the New York Auto Show sported large sliding glass. By the time the production 300 SL hit the streets, this had been be altered to a removable single-piece window that could be stored in provided pouches.

Although the hand-made racing spaceframe chassis would remain on the road-going 300 SL, Mercedes did make some

Fitted luggage for the rear deck was essential for journeys in a 300 SL.

Gas struts held up the 300 SL gullwing doors.

BELOW: **300 SL tubular spaceframe.**

changes so that the car would be more suitable for production. Since the company was no longer concerned about taking the 300 SL racing, the lightweight alloy body was swapped for a more conventional steel set-up. The boot, bonnet and gullwing doors were still made of aluminium, but everything else got considerably heavier.

Luxury items, road-legal safety additions and steel pieces made the street car weigh in at 2,855lb (1,298kg) a whopping 515lb (234kg) more than the racing machine. While this may seem like a lot, it still carried advantages in the consumer sports car community. The 300 SL weighed about the same as a 1954 Chevrolet Corvette, and that was running a six-cylinder engine with 65bhp less than the Mercedes. The Corvette and others would rise to meet the challenge of the 300 SL, but at its debut, the gullwing was the car to beat.

A couple of curious pieces did not make it on to the road-going 300 SL. Disc brakes were no longer the secret weapon of the British, and they could be fitted to any car. Still, Mercedes decided to stick to their well-proven drum brakes on their new premium sports car. Another racing piece that Mercedes decided was not ready for the road was the low-pivot single-joint swing rear axle that had been developed for the racing programme. Instead, the first road-going SL soldiered on with its original dual-joint racing unit. Two axles were available: a 3.64 that gave a top speed of 145mph (232km/h) and a 3.25 that topped out at 165mph (264km/h).

The 300 SL shares a stand with the 220 at London's 39th International Motor Show in 1954.

In the end, the process of becoming a road-legal sports car had taken the 300 SL from the scrappy underdog, which used luck and vigour to claim victory, to a brutish figure that weighed more but had larger muscles. In many ways, its brain had been developed too. Even without disc brakes or the new rear axle, the spaceframe chassis was revolutionary for a production model, and the 300 SL would be the first road car available with fuel injection. The 300 SL was about to enter new waters for the USA.

Racing Days

Production was delayed at Sindelfingen until August 1954, but the first 300 SLs were in the hands of American consumers before another year was out. These first customers were not looking for a car for popping down to the shops; they were lining up to purchase their very own Le Mans champion. This SL may have been made for the streets, but it quickly began to find its best home on the track. One successful American racer was Paul O'Shea, who won the Sports Car Club of America's production sports car championship in 1955 and 1956, piloting a new 300 SL.

Track time was not limited to members of the public who had bought a 300 SL. The car was becoming a good fit with the emerging GT racing class, and professional drivers were taking it on some of the most gruelling courses around the world. John Fitch, who drove the 300 SL race cars for Mercedes in 1952, won his class at the 1955 Mille Miglia. In fact, the 300 SL took all three GT podium positions at that race in Italy.

Fitch's co-driver for the Mille Miglia, Olivier Gendebien, also entered a 300 SL road car in the Liège-Rome-Liège rally in 1955. His victory behind the wheel of the Mercedes would catapult him into a career with Ferrari, and more wins. In 1956, the 300 SL even participated in the support race for the German Grand Prix, which had been won by the W194

The W198 was building its own racing reputation, including Paul O'Shea's 1955 sports-car championship in SCCA Class D.

The full 300 SL gullwing evolution: 1952 racer, 1953 prototype racer, 1954 production car, and 1955 SLR racing prototype built for Uhlenhaut.

race cars only 4 years earlier. Unfortunately, this time Mercedes would take only third place.

The Gullwing – The Social Butterfly

Mercedes-Benz's image in the USA had quickly returned after the Second World War to one of prestige and sporting status. This created an interesting time for the 300 SL. At $6,820 in 1954 (DM 29,000 at home in Germany), it was the most expensive Mercedes available, aside from the top levels of the 300 Series cars. It was double the price of a Jaguar XK120, so ownership of a gullwing sports coupé was a mark of high prestige.

The list of celebrities who owned 300 SLs included such luminaries as Clark Gable, Pablo Picasso and US publishing magnate William Randolph Hearst. Actor Steve

Mercedes-Benz 300 SL launch in Hollywood.

300 SL on its way to Max Hoffman's dealership in New York.

McQueen totalled one while filming *The Great Escape* in Germany. It also seems that Sophia Loren and Zsa Zsa Gabor overcame any worries about looking undignified while climbing over the high sills of the gullwinged car. When Max Hoffman hired famed architect Frank Lloyd Wright to design his Manhattan showroom, part of the payment was rumoured to be a 300 SL!

After the delay in production, Mercedes made only 146 examples of the 300 SL in 1954. However, in its first full year of production, Sindelfingen would put 867 more 300 SLs on the road. This would prove to be its peak year. When production ended, in 1957, a total of 1,400 gullwing coupés had been built. This included 29 special competition cars bodied in all-aluminium, which gave a weight saving of about 200lb (90kg). While all 300 SL coupés are much-desired collector items today, these very few alloy cars represent the upper echelon of these rare beauties.

W196 R AND THE 300 SLR

1954 was the year many at Mercedes had been waiting for since the company resumed production after the war. The 300 SL had skipped the 1953 season so that the Grand Prix car (codename W196 R) could be ready in time for 1954, when new rules would permit either 750cc supercharged cars or 2.5-litre naturally aspirated units.

Mercedes chose to build a new fuel-injected 256bhp 2.5-litre eight-cylinder motor to take on the world. The body would be either a streamlined open top or a monoposto, depending on the race, which also dictated inboard or outboard brakes and a wheelbase that was either 87 or 84.6in. Fangio and Kling scored a 1-2 victory at this car's first outing, at the French Grand Prix. The car would continue winning on the circuit and power was even upped to 290bhp for its second season.

Stirling Moss and Denis Jenkinson on their way to a record-setting win at the 1955 Mille Miglia driving a Mercedes-Benz Type 300 SLR.

Following its success in GP racing, Mercedes would apply many of the lessons of the W196 R into a new car for the 1955 World Sports Car Racing Championship. The engine was bored out to 3.0 litres, and the 300 SLR (W196 S) was born. Stirling Moss won the Mille Miglia in the 310bhp machine and went on to win the Tourist Trophy and the Targa Florio. 'No other car could possibly get near it', is how Moss remembers the quickness of the 300 SLR.

But, no matter how many victories it achieved in that year, this car would for ever be remembered for the tragic events at Le Mans.

The 300 SLR had such a hold on sports-car racing during the 1955 season that Jaguar knew its only chance of winning at Le Mans was to try and run hard enough to break the 300 SLR on the track. This heated competition, combined with a poor racecourse set-up, led to Pierre Levegh's SLR being launched into the crowd and the driver being killed. Track safety standards had barely altered since the first race more than 30 years earlier, when speeds had been much slower, and 83 spectators were also killed by flying debris. While Levegh was not blamed for this terrible accident, Mercedes chose to withdraw from the race out of respect for all the victims.

Even without Le Mans, the 300 SLR's victories brought it the overall championship for 1955. The W196 was a constant dominant force, too, winning nine out of sixteen Formula One races held over the 1954–55 seasons. Mercedes had now conquered the racing world with repeated triumphs and one crushing tragedy. They had proved what they set out to do, and now decided to focus once again on the business of making road cars. Mercedes' racing programme was formally retired during a public ceremony on 24 October 1955. The race cars were covered and the book on Grand Prix racing was closed; Neubauer wept.

Stirling Moss, Alfred Neubauer and Juan Manuel Fangio cover a W196 R at the end of the 1955 season.

CHAPTER FOUR

THE SL LOSES ITS TOP

The 190 SL premiered at the 1954 New York International Motor Sports Show, as the car that was just one step down from the 300 SL coupé.

Little Brother

The 300 SL was not alone on the Mercedes-Benz stand at the 1954 New York International Auto Show. Featuring next to the gullwing was a roadster that carried similar design cues but a smaller price tag. This attractive new model was the result of the inspiration of Max Hoffman, Mercedes-Benz's man in the USA, who also represented companies such as Jaguar and Alfa Romeo. He knew the American market enjoyed European roadsters, and it was he who had pressed Mercedes to produce a low-cost, high-style model to be the little brother to the 300 SL.

Mercedes obliged by reaching down into the more mass-produced side of the line-up to create a roadster. They started by shortening the platform of the 180 saloon so that the new car would have the same 94.5in wheelbase as the 300 SL. The design also carried a few of the curves of the upright Ponton from which it spawned, but the long nose, eyebrow lines over the wheels, and rounded rear were style touches unmistakably borrowed from the highly desirable 300 SL. The gullwing's new sibling would be known as the 190 SL.

The 300 SL experienced a delay from the New York show to production, but customers had to wait even longer for the 190 SL. The gullwing was in near-production form in New York, but the 190 SL was only a prototype. Mercedes had the car in testing from the auto show in February 1954 until the spring of 1955. In that time, the bonnet of the prototype changed from having an air induction scoop to a centre bump for clearance of the overhead cam cover. The bonnet's full length also originally ran down to the grille line much like Hobel, but was changed to accept a small panel – as had happened when the other SL car went into production. The initial base price in Germany was DM 16,500.

In addition to the fabric hood, a removable hard top was available, at first made of lightweight aluminium. After a switch to cheaper steel, the 190 SL's listing also changed, from roadster to coupé. While a removable hard top would not conventionally lead to a coupé classification, this would be a practice that Mercedes would continue.

Fritz Nallinger (right)
and Rudolf Uhlenhaut
(left) testing the 190 SL
(W121) prototype that
appeared at the 1954
New York International
Auto Show.

ABOVE AND ABOVE RIGHT: **Certain items changed from prototype to production 190 SL: the bonnet scoop was traded for a power bulge; the turning lights became round; and a panel was inserted between the grille and the bonnet.**

The appearance may have been sporty, but under the bonnet the car reflected its slightly more pedestrian roots. The 1.9-litre four-cylinder was a two-thirds variation of the inline six in the 300 SL, but with a shorter 83.6mm stroke and twin Solex carburettors instead of fuel injection. The 190 developed 105bhp (120bhp SAE in the USA) and a top speed of 106mph (170km/h). It was a great improvement over the 65bhp currently available in the 180 saloon, but it was a little awkward offering less than half of the power of Mercedes-Benz's other SL car.

Mercedes was getting more from its sub-2.0-litre four-cylinder engine than companies such as Triumph or Alfa Romeo were producing in their roadsters at this time. The problem was that the 190 SL tipped the scales on its own with the kind of weight the lower-powered cars achieved only when they were loaded with two passengers and a weekend's worth of luggage. Its 0–100km/h time was rated at 14.5 seconds (with two occupants), which lagged behind other open cars with similar displacements. The stats meant that the car was occasionally misunderstood as a portly sports roadster, but this new smaller SL was actually helping to defining a new sports-car genre at Mercedes-Benz.

TOP AND ABOVE: **The first hard tops were made of a lightweight alloy, but later ones had much improved rear visibility.**

TOM COTTER'S BARN FIND 1955 190 SL

I couldn't have been more than five years old, maybe six, when I got a ride in my first sports car. It was white with a black hard top and red interior, and had a stick shift. I can still see it in my mind's eye, more than half a century later. The car belonged to a friend of my Aunt Kiki, and it may, in fact, have helped make me become a lifelong sports car freak.

The car was a Mercedes-Benz 190 SL, and as opposed to many in the collector car world today, I do consider this a sports car. I love the way the car looks, the voluptuous curves of the fenders, the tail lights and the front grille. And I love its raspy little exhaust note. There is something just so correct about a 190 SL's proportions. Soon after my ride in the Mercedes, my dad bought me a Dinky Toy of the same car. I was smitten.

Years went by, decades really. In that time, I've owned nearly every sports car ever made. Seriously. MGTD, MGB, MG Midget, Triumph Spitfire, Porsche 356, Porsche Carrera S, Corvette Sting Ray, Sunbeam Tiger, AC Cobra, Datsun 240 Z, even a Cunningham C3, and many others. I loved them all. But there was always a void in my automotive bucket list.

Until a few months ago.

My passion since I was about 14 years old has been to discover barn-find cars; you know, cars that have been parked in a barn or warehouse or garage or field and forgotten. I've written a number of books about the subject, such as *The Cobra in the Barn*, and a few others. So I am always on the prowl for old cars and motorcycles as subjects for my next book.

Just like his books, Tom Cotter found a 190 SL in a barn.

Well, I was in Maggie Valley, North Carolina, last fall, and heard an urban legend; a guy named Steve Davis supposedly had hundreds of old cars and thousands of old motorcycles. I had to visit. Steve was a heck of a nice fellow, and told me he had been picking and collecting since he was a kid. He also told me he didn't usually sell anything. But he'd be glad to show me his fields and barns stocked with old cars. Fords, Studebakers, many old Jaguars, MGs, Volvos and more. But in one of his buildings, stored in a nice, dry corner, was a car that caught my attention: a dusty 190 SL. Steve told me it was a 1955, and that he had driven it there 20-some years ago. I said I'd be interested in buying it if he'd part with it, and he said yes, but only if I gave him signed copies of each of my books.

No brainer. He gave me the price and we shook hands on it.

A friend of Steve's, Eugene Smyre, also in the North Carolina mountains, picked up the car and is now restoring it for me. Eugene is no newcomer to the area of restoration, having restored, among others, the Mormon Meteor that won Best of Show at Pebble Beach and Amelia Island a few years ago.

So here I am, at 59 years old, about to be spiritually reunited with a car that turned me into a sports car geek so long ago. I wonder if the ride will be just as memorable.

What the 190 SL offered was Mercedes-Benz quality and comfort. In the important US export market it initially came in at $3,998. That was $548 over the quicker Jaguar XK-140 and $1,064 more than the Chevrolet Corvette, but the 190 SL came with proper side glass, a usable boot and a water-tight hood, something that was lacking on other contemporary roadsters. The 190 SL was a success for Mercedes because it offered a gracefully aggressive appearance in an affordable package that may not have been quick but was certainly sporting.

The 190 SL was not built merely to cash in on the company's reputation for good quality. Mercedes made sure it had the sort of sporting drive that its clientele expected from the three-pointed star. The rear suspension was fitted using Mercedes-Benz's latest innovation: the low-pivot swing-axle rear suspension. This was one area in which the 190 SL excelled over its larger gullwing brother. In fact, the suspension set-up was so well received that it would become a staple of Mercedes-Benz cars for the next few decades.

Because the 190 SL knew how to take a corner, Mercedes did all it could to turn it into a competition car. Lighter doors were made available, the windscreen could be swapped for a short racing model, and even the heavy chrome bumpers could be removed. This sports model was available from the

The exceptional handling of the 190 SL made it a contender at the 2012 Bahamas Speed Week Revival.

Douglas Steane won the 1956 Macao Grand Prix in his rare competition model (seen here outside a Mercedes-Benz dealer in Hong Kong).

factory, but it only found 10 takers. In the end, the 190 SL could look quick, but it was always outgunned in a straight line. Still, amateur racers did have some success with it, including Douglas Steane, who won the 1956 Macao Grand Prix in his lightened 190 SL, more than two laps ahead of the second-placed Ferrari Mondial 500.

Bigger Brother Loses Its Top

The 300 SL road car was competitive on the track, but on the street, the signature gullwing doors made it a bit intimidating to the average sports-car crowd. The quirky opening raised safety concerns about how driver and passenger might escape if the car found itself on its roof. In an era when exotic cars earned their name more through small-batch production, the 300 SL coupé was a true exotic, and that limited sales.

Max Hoffman once again approached Mercedes about the 300 SL, this time urging them to come up with a roadster with conventional doors and windows. The 190 SL had shown the potential of a folding hood and Mercedes may already have been thinking along the same lines: 300 SLs without a roof had been sketched just as the gullwing was hitting the market, and test cars had reportedly been seen in

ABOVE: **Clay model study for the 300 SL roadster. Items that were changed on the production model included the headlights and the shape of the rear fender.**

Rear of 300 SL roadster clay model, showing alternative rear end that carries elements from the front.

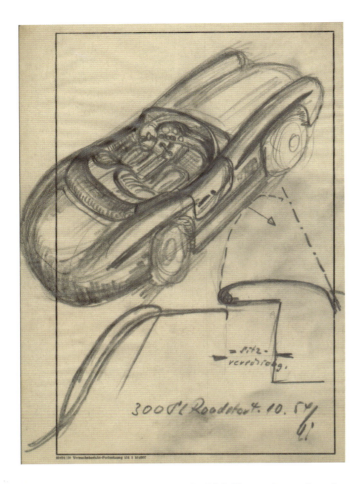

Friedrich Geiger's sketch of a 300 SL roadster dated October 1954.

Germany, possibly as early as 1955 and 1956. It was clear, too, that a few more creature comforts would be popular in the USA. Mercedes was keen on expanding its role in that market, so the designers set about removing the roof and adding more luxury to the machine that spawned from the near-racer known as Hobel. The car would be known as W198 II.

One element of the coupé would prove to be both the most significant asset and the toughest hurdle in creating the 300 SL roadster. The tubular chassis had been the entire reason the coupé needed its now-famous gullwing doors. The only way that Mercedes could provide traditional passenger openings would be to revise the middle of the chassis. The bars were cut down at the door frame and rigidity lost on the sides was made up by adding strength to the transmission tunnel in the middle. Now the car had room for lower sills and proper doors, with internal room for wind-down side windows.

Just as it was easy for Mercedes to create a few W194 racers for the 1952 race at the Nürburgring, the new roadster would be much easier to develop than the average car. The tubular chassis carried most of its strength below its roofline. Everything above the 300 SL's waistline was developed more for aerodynamics than for rigidity. This was a distinct advantage and would create one of the strongest roadsters of its time.

The roadster also provided Mercedes with an opportunity to improve on some of the gullwing's other shortcomings. The rear of the car was elongated by only about 2in (5cm), but that was enough, after a reshuffling of the gas tank and the spare tyre, to create usable boot space. The place behind the

300 SL roadster off its frame during restoration.

The 300 SL roadster's interior consisted of a driver's layout that would carry the fundamentals into its successor.

seats that had been for fitted luggage would now store the fabric hood. This was concealed by a one-piece hinged hard cover, which ensured no disruption of the roadster's beautiful lines. Inside, the gauges for fuel, coolant temperature and oil pressure were moved from below the speedometer and tachometer to a vertical stack in between the two dials – a style that was being utilized by the new Mercedes cars across the line-up.

The rear suspension was also taken into consideration. The 300 SL coupé had a swing-axle set-up that was more for professional racers when the car was at high speed. The more predictable low-pivot swing axle that was already enjoyed by less expensive cars in the Mercedes line-up was a welcome addition here.

The changes to the 300 SL were capped in the front with the new Bosch Lichteinheit arrangement. Now the headlight, fog light and indicator were all protected under a single glass housing. The effect seemed almost to be an extension of the 300 SL's tall, skinny fenders. Those in the USA did not get this

slick upgrade because uniform sealed-beam statutes required a more conventional headlight set-up for that market.

The upgrade to the roadster did come at a cost. In 1957 the new 300 SL convertible debuted at DM 32,500, a 12 per cent premium over the original coupé. In the USA, where the drop-top was specifically developed, the price jumped from $8,900 for the last of the gullwings to $10,970 for the first 300 SL roadsters. At least purchasers were getting more car for their money: it tipped the scales at 2,932lb (1,333kg), a 3 per cent increase over the coupé. The USA was given an extra 10bhp to try and offset this increase. In October 1958 a stylish and removable hard top was made available (a DM 1,500 option in Germany), which added another 88lb (40kg) to the car.

Maximum speed dropped from 165 to 155mph (264 to 248km/h), but the added weight was not the only reason for this. The W194's victories were based partially on its excellent aerodynamics, which came from a coupé. This was carried on in the gullwing, alongside flat panels underneath the car, which created a better slipstream. The roadster not

As the German economic miracle was taking hold, luxury goods like the 300 **SL** roadster were becoming accessible to more people in the home market.

300 **SL** W198 II fitted with a removable hard top and **US**-spec sealed headlamps.

only lost the airflow advantage of the gullwing's fixed roof, but its underside also lacked the panelling to channel the air. In addition, the 3.25 rear axle optional on the 300 SL coupé was not available on the roadster, which was given a 3.42 unit instead – the 300 SL roadster had a more obvious road-going purpose.

Celebrities flocked to buy the new roadster. Yul Brynner and Elvis Presley were noted owners and screen star Clark Gable owned both a gullwing and a roadster. *Playboy* founder Hugh Hefner identified his purchase of a white on black 1959 model as the point at which he began to live the *Playboy* lifestyle.

OWNER STORY – A SURVIVOR ROADSTER OVER A GULLWING

Langdon Wheeler's 1958 300 SL roadster.

Langdon Wheeler likes to drive his cars, and he found the ride of his 1955 300 SL gullwing too harsh (the double-joint swing axle is a suspected part of the problem.) So in 2002 he purchased a grey 1958 300 SL roadster with a red leather interior. This was a particularly special 300 SL considering it was over four decades old at the time of purchase, yet had been driven for just 7,040 miles in total. It had barely averaged more than an annual one-way trip from Stuttgart to Munich.

The story of this exceptionally low-use car starts with a true fan of the 300 SL who lived in Rochester, New York. He purchased a gullwing and a roadster to drive and a back-up car for each. His reserve roadster included features such as a high-performance camshaft, Rudge knock-off wheels, and a factory-installed ammeter below the dashboard. Possibly the most unique element was its colour: a shade of dark grey that was resprayed by the factory prior to delivery. After the death of the first owner, the car stayed within the family and continued to be used very rarely.

When Langdon Wheeler purchased the car it had been housed in Charlottesville, Virginia, and it had not left the barn very often. He appreciated the original condition of the car, but he was not going to keep a real driver's machine off the street. A year after he acquired the car, Wheeler's 300 SL had nearly 1,000 more miles on the odometer when it won the award for the Most Elegant Mercedes at the 2003 Amelia Island Concours d'Elégance.

OWNER STORY – A SURVIVOR
ROADSTER OVER A GULLWING *CONTINUED*

The interior looks almost as fresh as the day it left the factory.

A decade later, Wheeler's 300 SL roadster has about 15,000 miles on the clock. He explains the appeal of the roadster: 'The gear whine has gone (because Roadsters do not have the square-cut racing gears of the gullwing) and the high performance cam gives the Roadster much better power above 3,000rpm. The car truly "comes up on the cam" and starts to howl as the revs mount.'

Even though it had been used much more in recent years, 300 SL is still nearly factory-fresh. In 2012, it was brought to the Survivor Event, a show that specifically gives awards to cars that keep their original factory equipment – even new tyres count against participants. Langdon Wheeler's SL missed out on the top award, only because proving that his car was sprayed that special shade of grey by the factory is almost as hard as resisting a fair-weather joy ride in a 300 SL roadster.

Towards the End

While Mercedes adapted the 300 SL to add more creature comforts, other, more specialized manufacturers were adding horsepower to their vehicles. This was a particular problem when going racing. In order to compete with the extra power that other GT cars were getting on the race track, Mercedes decided to introduce a very limited edition model. The SLS was a 300 SL on a very strict diet. It had been stripped of the standard windscreen, all bumpers, the hood, and anything else that could be eliminated, saving a total of 840lb (382kg). The passenger side was then covered for better aerodynamics. Only two were produced. One went to Paul O'Shea, who once again captured the Sports Car Club of America's championship in 1957, this time in the more competitive, low-volume Class D.

While the gullwing would remain virtually unchanged during its lifetime, the roadster was improved with the times.

1957 Mercedes 300 SLS (Super Light Sport).

Mercedes was finally comfortable enough with disc-brake technology to upgrade the 300 SL to Dunlop units on all four wheels in March 1961. Some of the roadster's weight gain was reversed with the addition of an alloy block as standard in March 1962. These improvements would not be around for long, as production of both the 190 SL and 300 SL was ceased on 8 February 1963.

Mercedes and Hoffman seemed to have hit on the right formula for drop-top cars. Although sales were a bit slower for the convertible (1,858 built vs. 1,400 gullwings), the roadster was in production for twice as long as the gullwing. In addition, there was the 190 SL for all of the roadster's life. It sold 25,881 examples, making it the most popular SL to date.

As a pair, the 300 SL and the 190 SL represented the zenith of Mercedes-Benz's dual personality that it had cultivated most of its corporate life. At the top of the range, Mercedes offered exceptionally crafted vehicles that were engineering and aesthetic marvels, only accessible to the world's wealthiest and most powerful people. At the same time, there was a more budget-friendly line of cars that offered a taste of this prestige and build quality, wrapped in a less powerful package that was just distinctive enough not to dilute the company's premium image.

The 300 SL was the high-end model that borrowed pieces from Mercedes' top-of-the-line cars. There were also plenty of bespoke items available, such as the handcrafted chassis

Customers from the USA pick up 70 new Mercedes-Benz vehicles and tour Germany in May 1959 before having their cars shipped back home.

ABOVE AND ABOVE TOP: **The W198 II offered weather-tight high-speed motoring.**

that were built to ensure that this exclusive sports car kept to the highest standard.

The 190 SL represented the more economical end of the Mercedes line. It borrowed as much as it possibly could from the lower end of Mercedes cars, but it still carried a sizable price tag and an air of exclusivity. The 190 SL's welded unit body was not as elaborate as the 300 SL's tubular chassis, but it was still a premium idea in contemporary motoring. The next SL would bridge the strengths of the two convertibles into one car.

CHAPTER FIVE

W113 IS DEVELOPED

The 220 SE 'fintail' was the first car with a safety body and would provide the basis for a new generation of Mercedes-Benz cars.

Mercedes had gone through major changes during the time of the 300 and 190 SLs. The retirement of the W196 Silver Arrows had shut the door on the racing department, and the new buzzword was 'safety'. The saloon lines had gone from two distinct build methods to a strategy that merged the mid-level taxicabs and high-end celebrity favourites into one unibody. Technology, luxury and power represented the major class distinction.

The last Mercedes to have a separate body and frame was the 300 SL. While its tubular chassis was still an automotive marvel, it no longer had a place in the company. When the 300 SL gullwing was launched, in 1952, it had a power rating that was similar to that of the Ferrari 250s of the era. While Ferrari was able to spend the decade updating the power to

its 3.0-litre V12, Daimler-Benz was focused on expanding its entire line. Mercedes produced 108,440 passenger cars in 1959. It was the first time production broke into six figures (not counting commercial vehicles), and it meant that the company was producing more cars in one day than Ferrari was in a whole year.

The gap between the different types of manufacturer was widening. Mercedes recognized that the world of competitive sports-car racing now belonged to the specialist marques, and it could no longer spend resources developing powertrains for cars that would be produced only by the handful. The handcrafted tubular chassis design was too expensive to make just for a car that was not built to win at the race track.

Race in Oberschleißheim in 1962. The Ferrari 250 GT in the lead highlights the performance gap beginning to grow with the 300 SL.

The majority of Mercedes-Benz customers were not only interested in performance from the three-pointed star; they were also seeking the luxury associated with the company. The future of the SL lay in providing a good complement to the Mercedes road cars. The 190 SL had proven that a specialized sporting machine could be built utilizing as many production parts as possible, while still resulting in a car that was both driver-friendly and profitable. The next step now was to amplify the qualities of both SL cars.

Mercedes went about replacing the 300 SL and 190 SL with one vehicle, although, according to the company, 'both models represented two radically different design concepts and it turned out to be rather difficult to make out something like a common denominator'. Mercedes-Benz had always given the world practical cars as well as pleasurable driving machines. For the first time, its new sports car would offer both.

A Middle Starting Point

On 21 October 1958, Mercedes passenger car chief Fritz Nallinger signed off on the development of a sports car that offered improved spaciousness and touring comfort over the 300 SL. In Nallinger's view: 'There is no longer any need for the enjoyment of sporty driving to be physically strenuous.'

The rawness of the 300 SL would not be needed, and the agile tortoise of the 190 SL was not to be reproduced. Mercedes chose a middle ground to base their new SL, the 220 SE. The floorpan was shortened to give the same 94.5in that was found in both predecessors. This new car was given the code name W113.

Even without the 300 SL, there was still a 3.0-litre engine in the Mercedes line-up. The six-cylinder in the 300 SE could be traced back to origins similar to those of the 300 SL, but it was only making 160bhp in the luxury car. The W113 was a car for the world, and it did not need to be placed into the tax classes that this displacement would bring in many European countries. There needed to be a step down in exclusivity from the 300 SL, while at the same time creating a desire within the upper echelons of the middle class that was emerging in Germany and other parts of Europe. The 220 SE's engine, with a few alterations, would provide the right basis to achieve this goal.

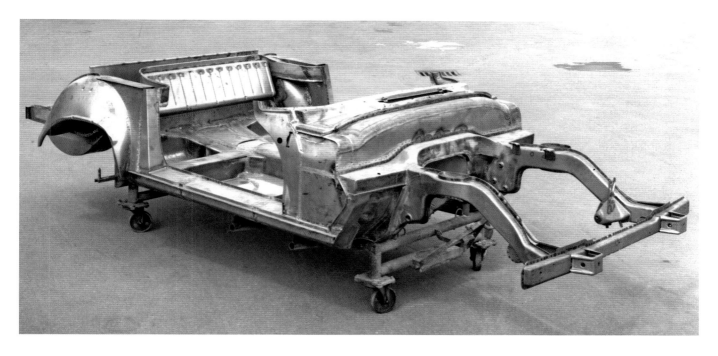

The 220 SE's pan adapted to make the W113 unibody floor assembly.

Barényi and Wilfert discuss safety with other Mercedes-Benz executives in 1960 (W113 design model on the left).

The original plans had the 220 SE's motor used as a direct transplant in the new W113 model SL; indeed, pictures do exist of near-final prototypes that wear the 220 SL badge. The 120bhp of the 220 SE would have provided a fine upgrade over the 190 SL, but the new W113 was living up to much more. Not only did it need to uphold some of the 300 SL's pedigree, but also the new safety features were going to make for a noticeably heavier car. In the end, the engine was reworked, including enlarging the displacement to 2.3 litres. This would place the new sports car out in front of its saloon/coupé cousins, and its extra muscle would rival the remaining 3.0-litre in power without paying the extra tax on more displacement.

Exterior Design

When the new project was first signed off, in the autumn of 1958, the preliminary sketches were far from ground-breaking.

The first ideas of the W113 body combined elements of the past by blending the style of the 300 and 190 SL roadsters. There was even a hint of the SLR in the fenders. As development continued, a car like this would have made for a classically attractive design, but it would not have lasted long amongst its peers.

The 1960s brought a design revolution, with elegance coming from subdued simplicity. Design lines would still flow the entire length of the car, but the fender no longer had to be the guiding line of the design. Grace and sophistication were being discovered in a clean theme that could be followed from headlight to brake light. Possibly the starting point was the Citroen DS in the mid-1950s but, by the next decade, this design approach was evident throughout the industry. The rolling waves of the Jaguar XK150 were replaced by the sleek lines of the E-Type. The scalloped fenders of the first generation of the Chevrolet Corvette were flattened into a Stingray for 1963. At Mercedes, the designers set about bringing the new SL in line with the modern times.

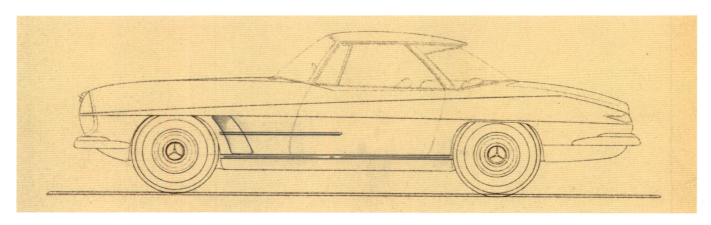

Early design sketch dated November 1958, showing influences from previous SL cars that would not make it into W113 production.

Styling sketch by Friedrich Geiger, dated February 1960.

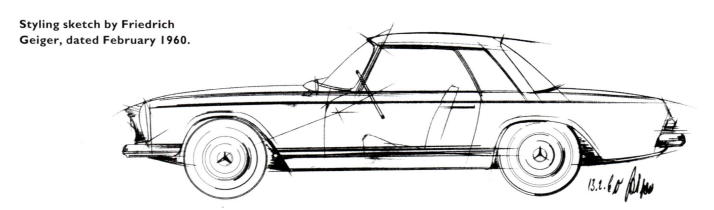

Friedrich Geiger was head of the Mercedes passenger-car styling department during this era, and he proved to be the right man for the job. He already had a connection with the SL, as the designer for the 300 SL gullwing and roadster, and was also known not to be particularly fond of using chrome in his designs. His ideas and approach would prove to be valuable in building a lasting SL for the 1960s.

Geiger had already laid the groundwork for a forward design on the W113. He brought the saloons into the 'fintail' era with the W111, but when he undertook the design for the coupé variant of the 220 SE and 300 SE models, he made sure that they carried a lower-profile rear end than their saloon counterparts. These luxury two-doors only had a hint of rise on the rear fender, which was seen more as an extension of the bodyline and not as a tailfin. While the fintails were a functional design element for parking, he recognized that they did not have to be an integral element for all Mercedes-Benz styling. Had the W113 carried tall, pointed rear fenders, it would have looked immediately outdated in essential markets such as the USA, where even Cadillac was downsizing its rear ends at this time. In fact, by the end of the 1960s, the Mercedes saloons would have adopted a rear that mimicked the W113.

As the sketching of the W113 continued, the project began to see function as a cornerstone of the design. The new car needed to occupy a similar footprint to the previous SL cars, but the aim was to offer a higher level of useful space and comfort. This began a theme of smooth surfaces that carried less trim and more integration.

Much of the W113 design team at work: Friedrich Geiger in the white coat and, left to right, Karl Wilfert, Fritz Nallinger and Paul Bracq.

Designer Paul Bracq began a journey to pen a car that was brand new but still distinctly Mercedes. Gone were the lines of the 190 SL, which tapered inwards from headlight to door handle. Instead, the W113 would be crisper, with consistent sides. The pontoon-like fenders of its predecessors were now replaced with a creased line that ran along the length of the car. Some prototypes show the W113 in a nearly complete form, but with the side vents borrowed from the 300 SL. These distracted from the simple elegance of the design and, had they been incorporated, the W113 would not have been allowed to stand properly on its own.

Some design sketches toyed with various radical styling features up front, but these did not make it to the modelling stage. In the end, the car would carry on the SL tradition of mounting the large tri-star emblem in the centre of the car. It now sat in the middle of a wider radiator grille, but it still maintained the family resemblance to the previous road-going SLs. Just like the 190 SL, the motor would be positioned upright, requiring one power bulge in the centre of the bonnet for clearance.

Mercedes was also now building its cars with vents directly in front of the windscreen. The company had become conscious about where its cabin air was originating, and the new placement kept it free from dust and fumes. This was a tradition that was started on the fintail cars and would continue on the new sports car. The central inlet hump near the base of the windscreen was far from overbearing. Instead, it was incorporated into the design as an extension of the power bulge. At the same time, it succeeded in giving the new car

A near-ready model. The production car would lose the panel below the front bumper and would have the new speciality tyres fitted.

BELOW: **Safety innovations included crumple zones.**

a unifying styling element that was carried on all premium Mercedes cars throughout the 1960s.

Convertible sports cars have always had a reputation for feeling a bit confined with the hood up, so special attention was given to providing a low waistline on the W113. This allowed for a larger area of glass, to give occupants a feeling of lightness and airiness without raising the car's height. The final touch of this plan for spaciousness relied on the use of thin pillars on the removable hard top, allowing in even more light.

Built into this new roadster were the latest safety innovations from Mercedes-Benz. Béla Barényi is considered to be the father of automotive passive safety, and he was spreading innovation across the Mercedes-Benz development department during the planning of the W113. Barényi

was a pioneer in building a car with a rigid cell passenger compartment surrounded by crumple zones. In the event of an accident, the system was designed to allow areas not carrying people to absorb the force of an impact, thus improving passenger protection. This made the W113 both safe and strong – a factor that would provide the car with a great advantage later in its lifecycle.

The integration of the extra comfort and safety features into this new car led to a significant weight gain. In order to preserve the sporting nature of the new sports car, the bonnet, boot-lid, door skins and tonneau cover were made from lightweight aluminium. This did not completely counteract the final product's hefty presence, but it did save the car from ballooning into a boulevard cruiser.

THE HEADLIGHT DIFFERENCE

US-spec headlights helped keep a visual link.

Federal Motor Vehicle Safety Standard No. 108 (FMVSS 108). It may not sound interesting, but it is significant – the reason why the W113 had a different set of headlights for the USA for its entire life.

The rest of the world had two distinct headlight models for the SL cars before the arrival of the W113. The 300 SL gullwing coupé had round headlights with the indicator light directly below the headlight unit. The 190 SL debuted during the era of the gullwing, and so it carried a similar headlight arrangement.

When Mercedes updated the 300 SL and made it into a roadster in 1957, the front-end styling changed. The corners of the car were given vertical Bosch Lichteinheit units that housed the headlight and indicator behind an oblong pane of glass. It was a pointer to the future of Mercedes-Benz's design language.

The USA never received the Bosch's vertical headlight enclosure, either on the W113, or on any saloons and coupés, because of FMVSS 108. Although it was created in December 1968, more than halfway through the W113's product life, FMVSS 108 united the USA's Society of Automotive Engineers (SAE) specifications that had been in place for three decades.

According to the National Highway Traffic Safety Administration, 'The headlamps available in the first third of the twentieth century were not nearly as reliable and as

THE HEADLIGHT DIFFERENCE *CONTINUED*

resistant to environmental degradation as headlamps today. Consequently, the replacement of headlamp parts was a persistent safety maintenance and inspection issue that concerned the states. This occurred because of the proliferation of hard to find replacement lenses, replacement reflectors and replacement bulbs. These were often not available at local service stations. Thus, in the US, the states agreed circa 1937 to adopt and standardize sealed beam headlamps technology, establishing interchangeability as specified in SAE standards as a top safety priority.'

The result was that all vehicles in the USA were required to have the same 7-in (178-mm) round headlamps. Later there would be a provision to make the quad lights (two per side) 5¾ in (146mm) optional, but during the development of the 300 SL roadster the dual set-up was the only one that was legal.

From a design standpoint, this meant that Mercedes could not use the oval shape to hide the headlights when it created the 300 SL roadster. In order to comply with FMVSS 108, the lights had to be round and exposed, giving the US-market SL cars an interesting look. 300 SL roadsters destined for the USA were fitted with a chrome plate that located the headlight at the top and the indicator directly below it. Although the indicator shape was much larger than on the 300 SL gullwing and 190 SL, it gave the US-bound 300 SL roadsters a much stronger visual connection to the other two cars.

The Bosch Lichteinheit headlamps from the 300 SL roadster were purposely carried over into the W113 to help bridge the SL design legacy. Once again, a different light housing would be needed for the USA. A similar headlight fix was applied to US-bound W113 cars, with the housing made of glass instead of chrome.

These new headlights carried a part number LE 1657 AC in the USA – a distinction that would prove to be important later in the life of the W113. This not only provided an economical solution to a US-specific regulation, but it also continued the visual connection established in the USA. The headlamps in the USA may have created a stronger link across the entire SL line, but the round units made the W113 look more traditional. The USA missed out on what was arguably one of Mercedes-Benz's greatest styling touches.

US-spec headlights on a 300 SL and a late-series W113.

The Pagoda Roof

Safety guru Béla Barényi had discovered that a concave design could add extra strength and had patented the roof shape in 1956. His view was that it could offer occupants more safety and allow the roof to safely carry larger loads. Other benefits would include extra headroom and better visibility from the taller windows.

Barényi decided to test his idea out with a small saloon. The K 55 project was a three-box design, with the bonnet and boot having a similar shape and size, giving the car a peculiarly symmetrical profile. Its squared-off lines offered exceptional interior room, and Barényi demonstrated the concave roof's strength by using it for extra storage. While

BELOW: **The W113 series with a 'pagoda' roof in place before safety testing.**

RIGHT: **Patent for Barényi's symmetrical car, including rigid roof design.**

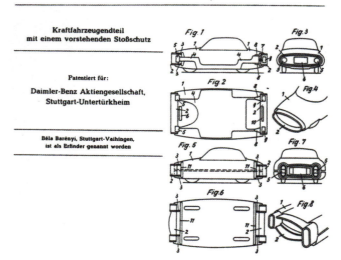

ABOVE AND BELOW: **Design study that showed the W113 beginning to take its final shape. It is notable that this one has '220 SL' still on the boot (indicating that plans for engine enlargement were not yet finalized), and does not have the production car's now celebrated concave roof. This near-final model also had provisional elements such as the door handles from the 300 SL and a sloping doorline that gave the rear fender a more pronounced wing.**

this was a humble saloon, the spaciousness and strength lessons learned from the concept would soon be applied to something a little sportier. Friedrich Geiger was looking for original style for the new SL, and Paul Bracq was able to incorporate Barényi's concave roof into the organic design that was becoming the W113.

Some of Bracq's early sketches for the roof included two parallel metallic strips that ran along near the edge of the roof, joined with the c-pillar, and then seamlessly connected with ornamental metal strips that ran down the boot to the taillight. It was an inescapably odd design element and would eventually be toned down to just the roof, where it could serve as a functional space to hold an optional roof rack. The result of this more restrained form was something that is now legendary, but it was considered to be quite controversial at the time, as the designers were still working towards final approval from the Mercedes board.

Geiger was not the only one who helped to push this roof design through. He was aided and abetted by one of Barényi most friendly allies, Karl Wilfert. As head of bodywork design and testing, Wilfert often had to make practical decisions, but his reasons for supporting the concave roof may not have been entirely rooted in engineering. His assistant during this era was Werner Breitschwerdt, who would eventually become Chairman of the Board of Management of Daimler-Benz AG. According to Breitschwerdt, his boss was at his happiest when the designs sparked some debate. 'Imagine a modern sculpture – people stand around and argue about it until they are blue in the face. That was to Wilfert's taste. The fact that one had to discuss it – that appealed to Wilfert.'

Wilfert might have had a very good point with the W113. The roof became such a discussion point that it quickly dictated the car's nickname. Another Daimler-Benz board member, Hans Scherenberg, later acknowledged that the W113's development may have been a case of style over substance: 'The Pagoda was a special trademark more than anything – it didn't actually have any purpose in terms of the car's engineering.'

Although the concave roof created some initial internal controversy, there was one argument that often quelled serious opposition. Because the new SL was designed from the outset to be available with a fabric top as well as a removable metal top, anyone who did not like the look could simply erect the traditionally shaped soft hood. The argument was won, and the hard-top design was approved with the iconic 'pagoda' concave lines.

Near-final W113 interior on a late-series prototype.

Interior Design

From the standpoint of the driver, there were many similarities between the 230 SL and the 300 SL Roadster. The W113 borrowed the gauge layout from its predecessor, which included a large tachometer to the left, a large speedometer to the right, and in the centre a vertical stack that gave information on fuel level, oil pressure, coolant temperature and

Safety wedge-pin door locks.

battery charge, and included the instrument dimmer switch. This may not seem like much, but the set-up was simpler and easier to read than the set of gauges provided on the lower part of the dash that was standard in the 300 SL gullwing and the 190 SL.

On a late prototype, the fresh air vents were just cross-hair grates that conformed to the shape of the dash panel ends. By the time the car reached production, they had been upgraded to more stylish round units that fitted much better with all the other rounded elements of the dash (tachometer, speedometer, clock, ignition barrel, and so on). This final design also allowed for a window defroster and vent shut-off slider.

This same prototype also located the speedometer to the left of the central gauge cluster and the tachometer to the right. This arrangement never reached production. All cars

go through many minor improvements before reaching mass production, but it is worth noting that Mercedes did sell some of the final pre-production W113 cars. Keen collectors out there may want to pay close attention to any apparent oddities found on early cars.

Barényi's safety innovations were also evident in the interior. The doors were given his new wedge-pin locks that featured two safety catches. This was to keep the passenger safety cell intact, by preventing the car door flying open on impact. This feature also prevented the jettisoning of occupants during an accident. Barényi was also behind the idea to move the steering gear from the front section of the car back into the firewall. This would help prevent the steering column pushing into the driver during a frontal collision. The feature was innovative for its time and would be improved even further during the W113's lifecycle.

BÉLA BARÉNYI

Béla Barényi in his private archive.

Béla Barényi was a free-thinking engineer who became the father of passive safety. He first joined Mercedes-Benz in time to work on its entry-level Type 170 V convertible. Although less expensive, the body welded to the platform seemed to provide more side protection than the x-frame of the larger cars. This was just at the beginning of the Second World War, so there was little time to devote to further research.

After the end of the war, Barényi started to work on his own vision of a vehicle for the future. His Terracruiser featured six seats, with the driver sitting in the front centre position. It pioneered a new idea in protection, with a strong passenger compartment connected to more deformable cells that could absorb the force of an impact in the front or rear. His three-passenger Concadoro also placed the driver in the middle, and was notable for its design features, including a padded steering wheel, recessed windscreen wipers, and a safety steering column. According to Mercedes: 'Barényi's Concadoro bodywork design was much further advanced than the bodies of all of the Mercedes-Benz models of the early post-war period.'

Barényi returned to Mercedes-Benz in 1948. He immediately got to work designing a stronger floor assembly for the upcoming W120 Ponton saloon line. In 1953 he was transferred to the development department at Daimler-Benz, where he integrated his work with the Terracruiser ideas to further develop safety at Mercedes. The 1959 W111 saloon (later known as the 'fintail') was the first production car with a passenger safety cell surrounded by crumple zones. Other Barényi safety innovations featured on the fintail saloons, including the collapsible steering column and the padded steering wheel. The car also featured a wedge-pin door lock that would keep the doors closed in the event of an accident, helping to maintain the integrity of the passenger safety cell.

Since the W113 Pagoda SL was based on the design of the W111 220 SE, Barényi had an established base on which to work his safety magic. The W113 was developed not only with the innovations of the W111, but also some more unique elements, such as the pagoda-style concave roof. As the first safety-conscious sports car, the 230 SL was ahead of its time.

Barényi's idea – to protect the occupants in a rigid frame, and design areas outside the passenger compartment to bear the brunt of any impact – was revolutionary at the time and is still a part of automotive engineering today. The concept of crumple zones was just one safety innovation of his that was adopted far and wide; the ideas of the Concadoro have also been implemented recently in Daimler's diminutive smart roadster. Barényi's work had a profound influence on Mercedes, and indeed the entire industry, that was felt long after he retired from Mercedes, in 1972. Barényi died on 30 May 1997 with 2,500 patents to his name and his picture in the Automotive Hall of Fame.

The Terracruiser was an early study in safer car construction by Barényi that would evolve into systems used on the W113.

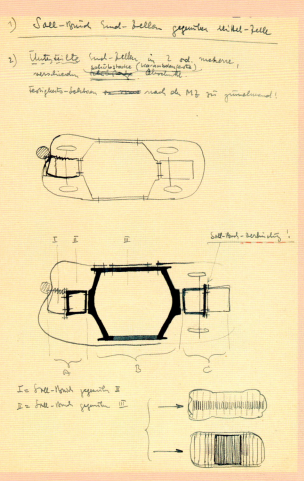

January 1951 – patent # 854 157 is taken out by Daimler-Benz for the rigid passenger safety cell (this is Barényi's sketch for this principle). The W113 would be the first production sports to apply this standard.

Chassis Set-Up

Inevitably, a certain amount of compromise went into the development of the W113, but Mercedes always had one ace up its sleeve to ensure that the car would live up to its heritage. Rudolf Uhlenhaut, the father of the original SL racer, was head of passenger-car development, so the W113 would pass through his hands.

Good dimensional planning was a priority and the company turned again to the 94.5-in wheelbase, the seemingly magic number that allowed for good manoeuvring and stability. Ferrari would also trust this length for its short-wheelbase sports cars during this era. The W113 was given a wider front and rear track (58.5in) to help keep a solid road feel.

The swing-axle rear suspension from the 300 SL roadster and 190 SL would also be utilized on the W113. Each wheel could move independently from the others, as a single hinge mounted low on the rear differential joined the two axle sections. This low-pivot swing axle also incorporated a transverse compensation spring to ensure uniform wheel alignment during hard cornering.

A rear swing axle might not have been the most advanced piece of machinery at the time, but it was something that had been proven by Mercedes engineers to be safe and secure. The low pivot point and compensating spring were two small elements that made it a superior set-up. Mercedes applied this science to give its larger, heavier saloons a comfortable ride without creating a cushioning effect that risked a loss of road feel. This was the hallmark of Mercedes' cars, and similar principles would be applied to the W113.

Up front was an independent suspension, made up of unequal-length double wishbones, coil springs and gas shocks. The major components were borrowed directly from a 220 SE, then tuned to tighter sports-car specifications. Development plans also included an automatic gearbox – a first for a SL. The engine and transmission had three mounting points to attach to the subframe. That full front subframe then bolted to the unibody at three mounting points. The saloon/coupé origins were not completely engineered out of the W113, which offered a balance of sports-car handling without a harsh ride – a combination that was unheard of during this era.

Finally, one major component that was often overlooked in other cars, but was essential in the W113, was the tyres. Although the W111/W112 rode on 13-in cross-ply rubber, it was decided that the W113 would utilize some radial tyre technology. Radials could reduce friction while providing the car with a wider grip area, but Mercedes was not quite ready to give up the better ride quality of the cross-ply.

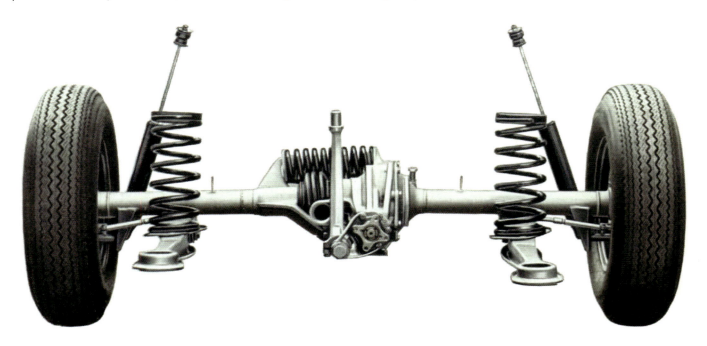

W113 rear suspension.

W113 front subframe.

Special rubber from Continental and Firestone was requested. The cords in these 14-in tyres struck a balance between radials and cross-ply by being offset from the tread by 10 degrees. This meant that they had good low-speed comfort while still having some flex to keep the tread in contact with the road during high-speed manoeuvres. They also had a rubber bead that protruded slightly from the tyre base, which served as a protective strip against curb damage. The grip of these special tyres was part of the tuning that brought together the handling characteristics of the short wheelbase and independent suspension.

CHAPTER SIX

230 SL

Béla Barényi (right) and Paul Bracq at the launch of the 230 SL at the 1963 Geneva Motor Show.

Introducing the 230 SL

The Mercedes 230 SL was first introduced to the world on 15 March 1963 at the Geneva Motor Show. Almost instantly, the unique shape of the roof had the press referring to the car as the 'Pagoda'.

Unlike today, when the omnipresence of camera phones has turned everyone into a spy photographer, and the abundance of online information forces more disclosure, in 1963 a new car could be a genuine surprise. A new SL had been rumoured but, aside from some glimpses caught as the car was testing in the months before Geneva, the 230 SL was a fresh face.

As car magazines were getting their first glimpse of Mercedes' new Pagoda, their excitement sometimes caused misinformation. Although a few had preview drives, most were not able to give much more than a few pictures and statistics sheet. In fact, some magazines accidentally published the information that this in-between sports car was designed to bridge the gap between the 190 SL and the 300 SL, not replace both of them.

Part of this confusion came from the fact that, although Mercedes had been able to show the 230 SL to the world at Geneva, that did not mean it was ready for production. There was still more engineering needed to get the 230 SL up to the exacting standards of Mercedes-Benz. Supplier delays also pushed back series manufacturing into the summer. The first

ABOVE: **Home launch of the Mercedes-Benz 230 SL at the International Motor Show Frankfurt, September 1963.**

230 SL debut at the International Motor Show Frankfurt, September 1963.

production 230 SL did not roll off the assembly line at Sindelfingen until July 1963. The first sales were in Germany, where the purchase price for the new model started at DM 20,600.

Mercedes sold nearly half its cars outside Germany at this time, and so reaching export markets was high on the company's 'to do' list. The first 230 SLs began to reach dealers in North America by autumn 1963, starting at $6,343 (plus $100 for delivery to the West Coast). They followed up in the UK in November 1963. These early right-hand drive cars were a little odd due to the deletion of the side mirror. Mercedes only equipped the first batch of 230 SLs with driver-side mirrors for LHD cars, and markets like the UK were better off waiting until after the spring of 1964 when right-side mirrors began to appear on the option list.

Sindelfingen factory in the mid-1960s.

ABOVE, ABOVE RIGHT AND OPPOSITE TOP AND BOTTOM: **Although the same height of the 190 SL and within an inch of the 300 SL roadster, the W113's large glasshouse made it sometimes appear to stand tall.**

Standard equipment included a four-speed manual transmission, fog lights (later versions optional), lockable glovebox (same key as the boot), MB-Tex vinyl seating, and a fuel cap unlocked with the door key. Although it seems a bit strange for a car of this calibre, there was no standard radio for the W113. In fact, the Pagoda cars were often photographed without any radio option because the plate used to cover the centre slot was a handsome metal fitting sporting the 230 SL badge in chrome (and the 250 SL and 280 SL badge on later cars). This was a design characteristic of both the 190 SL as well as the contemporary Mercedes saloons, with which the 230 SL shared many components.

Other options included power steering, leather interior, seatbelts, fitted luggage, and chrome strips on the hard top that allowed a ski rack to be mounted. A transversely mounted seat was also available from the outset, with the rear occupant sitting on the left side of the car (regardless of market) and his or her legs given a footwell behind the right-hand seat.

The 230 SL was sold as a roadster, coupé or convertible, but the 230 SL was not quite as distinct as that range might imply. The roadster had the soft top only; the coupé was sold with the removable hard top but no soft top; and the convertible was sold with both tops.

Early 230 SL interior including body-coloured side vent panel surrounds and fully round chrome horn surround on the steering wheel.

The tonneau cover mounted flush with the body and stored the soft top out of the passenger cabin.

The set-up and interchangeability of the three models were conveniently simple. As on the 300 SL roadster, the soft top was stored under a hard tonneau cover that mounted flush with the car's body. This allowed the hard top to be placed directly over the soft top mounting when the fabric top was stowed. Coupés could also have the ragtop and cover retrofitted at a later date.

The system gave 230 SL owners good flexibility – a roadster owner could later purchase the hard top, and it would already be set up for use on the car. Coupé owners could later buy a soft top and have it easily fitted on their Pagoda, so that it looked as if it had come that way from the factory. No one customer ever had to make a permanent decision on his or her W113's classification – with one exception (see Chapter 9).

Pricing for these three models was pretty simple. The roadster was the base model and came in at DM 20,600. If a hard top was purchased to create the range-topping convertible, it was an additional DM 1,100. For those who wanted the mid-level coupé, DM 750 was refunded for deleting the cloth top.

The New 2.3-Litre

The engine was the inline six-cylinder four main bearing unit lifted from the 220 SE. The bore was increased by 0.079in (20mm), and the extra 111cc took the engine to 2306cc. The changes did not end there. The cylinder head was swapped for a new alloy unit that allowed the compression ratio to be

increased from 8.7 to 9.3. The valves were larger than on the 220 SE, and the camshaft was modified. The 230 SL's engine also had the distinction of being the first Mercedes to use an alternator instead of a generator.

The two-plunger Bosch injection pump used in the 220 SE was replaced with a Bosch system that utilized a separate plunger for all six cylinders. Unlike the Mercedes saloons, the fuel injection was moved from the intake manifold to the cylinder induction ports, which allowed it to be pre-heated for better efficiency. This was not as advanced as the cylinder-wall injection system on the 300 SL, but, with the phasing out of that car, the 230's injection would become the most advanced available in the Mercedes family.

All of these upgrades yielded an extra 30bhp, bringing the 230 SL's total to 150bhp (DIN). The torque increased by 4lb/ft to 144lb/ft at 4,500rpm. Of course, this was interpreted a little differently, depending where the car was sold.

While DIN and SAE power ratings only have a little bit of variation, German DIN measurements utilized to advertise Mercedes products through most of the world rate net horsepower. In the USA, SAE ratings are taken from an engine's net horsepower, which means that the American muscle cars of the same era were advertised at stratospheric horsepower ratings. The 230 SL was therefore rated at 170bhp and 159lb/ft in the USA, apparently gaining 13 per cent more power and 11 per cent more torque as soon as it came off the boat!

It is worth noting that the 230 SL's engine involved far more than just a few bolt-on upgrades to the 220 SE. *Car and Driver*, in its June 1963 preview of the 230 SL, was impressed: 'The

The 2.3-litre injection engine M 127 II of the 230 SL.

230 SL Bosch fuel-injection system.

The engine M127 II (type 127.981) motor was a snug fit in the engine compartment.

exhaust valves are sodium-cooled and made from an alloy high in nickel content, the stems are chrome plated and the guides are of bronze to aid heat dispersal, the seats are "armoured" and an automatic device rotates the valve in relation to its seat every time it is opened.'

This attention to detail reflected the fact that Mercedes knew the new SL would often be driven hard. It may not have had the same power as its competitors, but it could keep up better than expected because it would perform flawlessly even when driven at its limits.

Mercedes buyers today expect perfection, but the set-up on the new SL was not without its faults. The motor was a model of reliability, but running an engine hard can bring a fair amount of noise. Also, the fuel-injection system sometimes needed a few winds as it primed before firing, especially on a cold start.

Gearbox, Drivetrain and Chassis

The four-speed manual transmission on the 230 SL was borrowed from the Mercedes parts bin. Instead of reaching for the 220 SE's bag, as they had when considering many of the other parts, this one came from the upmarket 300 SE. Using a taller first gear than on the saloon, the internal gear ratios for the manual were 4.42 for first, 2.28 for second, 1.53 for third, and 1.00 for fourth.

Although a tall first gear became more usable, some felt it was not matched correctly for enthusiast driving because the gearbox was developed for the more powerful 300 series vehicles. *Car and Driver* gave its opinions in June 1963: 'First gear is very short and runs the engine out of revs at 30mph; it is only the marvellous flexibility of the engine that prevents a dying gasp as second gear is engaged. The drop

Four-speed automatic transmission staggered shift gate.

ABOVE: **A white car with white-wall tyres made for a popular publicity shot for Mercedes-Benz during the early months of the 230 SL, but it is believed that very few German customers took that particular tyre option.**

power (though torque doesn't peak until 4,500rpm) but we would counter that it is precisely on such an engine that a close-ratio gearbox is at its best.'

Part of the Mercedes corporate argument for this transmission was its ease of use for those who did not want to change gear quite as much. With this gearbox, it was offering decent flexibility for the more luxury-minded crowd, with an ability to run from 10 to 125mph in fourth gear. Despite its defence of this set-up, however, Mercedes did eventually alter its approach.

While the manual gearbox had the capacity for less driver interaction, the automatic transmission was unique in the level of driver involvement it still demanded. It was a floor-mounted automatic, laid out in an erratic pattern listed in descending order as 2-3-4-0-R-P (0 as neutral). A four-speed

from second to third is well spaced, but while third is good over 80mph, there is an annoying gap between it and fourth. Mercedes-Benz might argue that a close-ratio gearbox isn't necessary with an engine of the 230 SL's low-speed pulling

planetary gearbox with fluid coupling, from its operation, it offered three distinct forward modes.

Selecting '4' on the lever would have this transmission behave like a conventional automatic, shifting its way to top gear. Selecting '3' worked in a similar fashion to '4', except that the car would not shift into its highest gear. Both of these would up shift at relatively low engine speeds as long as the car was not being driven hard (2–4 gears could be delayed to as much as 5,800rpm under heavy acceleration and held manually to the 6,500rpm red line).

What was most noteworthy about these two modes was the fact that the car would start off in second gear. Suppressing first gear was nothing new in the world of automatic transmissions. It just added weight to the contention that a sports car should not have an automatic gearbox at all. The only way to get a first-gear start, without mashing the accelerator pedal for a forced kickdown, was by selecting '2'. This would start the 230 SL in first gear and shift into second gear when the engine had built up enough speed. From there, the driver could manually shift into higher gears as needed.

Given this ability and encouragement to manually shift the automatic transmission, the reason for the erratic pattern of the shift quadrants became a bit clearer. If the layout had been one straight line of available modes, it could have led to missed gears or attention being taken from the road. The non-linear shift pattern allowed for quick changes between gears that could confidently be performed by touch.

Mercedes provided an 'Automatic' badge on the rear of every car optioned for that transmission outside of North America. Aside from clearly telling the world that the driver did not manually change gear on his or her sports car, the penalty for selecting the four-speed automatic was minimal. The auto gearbox did not represent a significant weight

Mercedes modern sports car highlighted by a modern German building.

A German advertisement mentioning the safety and security suspension elements of a 230 SL.

gain over the standard four-speed transmission, and the top speed of 121mph (194km/h) meant that the automatic was almost as fast as the manual. In fact, flexibility of the automatic created acceleration runs that were nearly as quick as (and sometimes quicker than) the manual transmission. The auto/manual debate would finally be put to rest later in the 230 SL's life.

When it came to stopping, the 230 SL was initially given 10-in 252-mm) Girling disc brakes up front, which had first made an appearance on the 220 SE. The rear brakes were 9.1in (230mm) Al-fin drums. While this braking set-up may seem inferior today, it was ideal for Mercedes, which was relatively new to incorporating disc-brake technology in their passenger cars.

The set-up had the security of two separate circuits running the front and rear brake units. The discs had the better stopping power up front, where more of the SL's weight was distributed – the front/rear distribution was 53/47. The drums were better at holding the parking brake when settled on hilly terrain. The control for the parking brake was located on the left side of the transmission tunnel. Contrary to initial pre-production reports, this position was not altered for right-hand drive models.

On the road all the elements of the 230 SL achieved the recipe that the engineers were looking to create. While the low-pivot rear swing axle emphasized handling and reduced unsprung weight, there were comfort items too, such as the steering damper rod that absorbed bumps in the road before they could be transmitted through the steering wheel.

The combination meant that the first reviewers of the new sports car were feeling capability rather than harshness. The reporter for *Autocar* in 1964 was impressed: 'Corners can be taken at almost prodigious speeds with extraordinary stability, ease of mind and control, and there is no apparent body sway to emphasize just how hard the car is being cornered. A closed circuit and a skilled driver are needed for its limits to be approached, while for ordinary fast road use there is a wide safety margin for misjudged bends entered too fast. The Firestone Phoenix tyres fitted must also play an important part in the fine handling; but they do squeal fairly readily. The 230 SL contradicts those who maintain that a swing-axle independent rear suspension must result in oversteer in certain circumstances.'

Tyres can often be an overlooked part of development, but as the magazine article mentioned, they were an essential element for the 230 SL. Uhlenhaut's request to Firestone and Continental for specialty rubber was paying off with the

Firestone Phoenix tyre, special to the W113. On two-tone cars, the body-coloured steel wheel never changed even with second colour on the centre cap. This created an interesting contrast for some cars with multiple layers of colour and chrome occupying the 14in wheel area.

press and Mercedes-Benz customers. The 14in low-profile tyres were a key to the Pagoda's harmony.

The 230 SL floorplan was relatively unchanged from those used in the saloons, although the set-up was strengthened and shortened for a better feel. It was an efficient way to avoid an expensive bespoke chassis, such as that on the 300 SL, at the same time creating a vehicle that would be more sporting than the 190 SL. In fact, the W113 was 40 per cent stiffer than the 190 SL.

Rigidity was a key feature of this chassis and it was demonstrated on an early promotional film featuring Mercedes race team driver Karl Kling. Having parked the car on an uneven surface with each of the wheels at a different elevation, he was still able to open and close the coupé's doors repeatedly without any problem. While watching a racing driver operating doors did not exactly make riveting television, it did emphasize the advantage of welding the body on to the floorpan to create a monocoque in an era when some sports cars were still a body bolted to a frame.

The attention to firmness came at a price. The 230 SL tipped the scales at 2,855lb (1,295kg), nearly 300lb (135kg) more than the 190 SL. Indeed, it was only able to retain the *Leicht* part of

These stills from a *c.*1963 promotional video show celebrated Mercedes racer Karl Kling demonstrating the new 230 SL, showing off the unibody strength and suspension capabilities, and the benefits of the swing axle.

its name owing to the extensive use of aluminium, and it continued to live up to the *Sport* part of its name because it offered a 43 per cent horsepower increase over the 190 SL. This extra power helped to compensate for the extra girth, and gave the 230 SL a better power-to-weight ratio than the 190 SL.

Interior

The experience of stepping in to the 230 SL was quite similar to that of getting into any other contemporary passenger Benz. The long, thin dash panel that followed the curve of the windscreen was the standard issue for all of the cars during that time. The 230 SL retained the circular clock, floor-mounted gear stick and body-coloured metal dash panel of the previous SLs. The larger coupés and saloons used rectangular clocks and more wood panels throughout the dash. Although wood trim was considered a luxury item,

an enhancement to any car, the lacquer paint on the minimalist dash gave the 230 SL a very Italian appearance (but without losing the typically German feel of quality).

One of the most important distinctions for the driver between the SL and its saloon cousin was the lack of the vertical set-up for the driver instruments. Instead, the 230 SL received a more informative evolution of the 300 SL's instruments, with round gauges for the speedometer and tachometer. This was considered to be an improvement and, during the lifetime of the W113, Mercedes would phase out the vertical stack on the saloons and give them a similar look to the SLs.

Mercedes-Benz's new commitment to safety meant that every interior surface was built to deal with an occupant potentially coming into contact with it. For example, the rear-view mirror frame would break cleanly away when under pressure, the heater controls would bend when forced against the metal backing, and the window cranks

The seats were particularly noted for comfort and good adjustment.

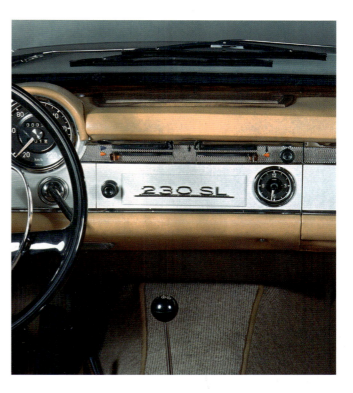

ABOVE: **Dual heater controls were a standard luxury feature.**

Optional Becker Europa radio.

Both doors had armrests and door pockets, and the passenger-side doors had a grab handle.

BELOW: **The seat backs had ventilation for longer-term comfort.**

were malleable, in case any part of a driver's or passenger's leg was caught on it during an impact. Although they were safe and soft, these pieces did not lose functionality or reliability.

The steering wheel was similar to the one available in the 300 SL and 190 SL. It was a large and skinny plastic control with a chrome inner ring. Unlike its predecessors, the two-spoke design ran straight across the wheel and there was less brightwork. The centre cap was larger than on the previous SLs to allow for safety padding. It was available in black and could be switched to white as a no-cost option. Initially, there was not a listing for the ivory wheel, but road tests in multiple publications using pre-production cars show that the white wheel was utilized from the start.

Just within reach of the steering wheel was a multi-functional stalk, branching out from the left side of the steering wheel column. This was moved up or down to trigger the indicator lights, which were then cancelled by the steering. Pushing outwards engaged the windscreen wipers until the lever was released, and normal wiper operation involved

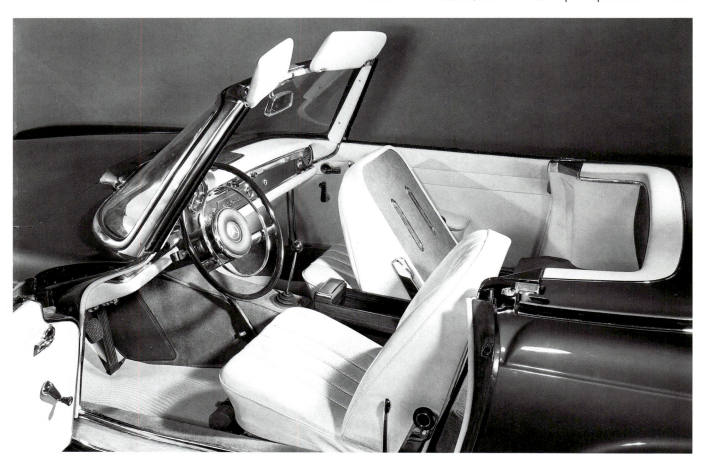

pushing the stalk in and adjusting the speed with the rocker switch. Switching from bright to dimmer headlamps was as simple as pulling back on this same lever. It may all seem commonplace now, but this kind of simplicity was new to drivers in 1963. In fact, it was so radical that the bright/dimmer switch was also located on the footwell, to conform to US standards.

Part of the luxury feel came from the engineer's attention to keeping fresh air flowing through the car. The driver and passenger had separate heating and vent controls. On each side there was a dedicated defrost vent next to each occupant vent. Air conditioning was an option that was available via a separate unit that mounted under the dashboard. This was a popular choice in the warmer areas of the USA.

Getting the air in the car was one thing, but the W113 also had a nice trick to get it out: a perforated surface on the coupé roof that allowed air to pass through. This flow was then channelled through an opening above the rear window that was shielded by a small overhang. The result was a constant airflow that did not allow any wet weather to pass back through it.

Ventilation was also a staple for the seats in the 230 SL. The perforated seat surface worked in conjunction with the vents at the rear of each chair to keep occupants feeling fresh. The seats with airflow had been seen in the 300 SL's sport buckets,

230 SL with side-vent panel surround in chrome. The car also came with a passenger-side windscreen sticker informing the driver of gear shift points and service intervals.

but the ventilation found a much better home in the grand touring seats of the W113. This may not seem like a significant point, but it was important for the long-term comfort of a driver. *Motor* magazine's review in June 1965 was very complimentary on this subject: 'Fortunately, the ergonomists at Stuttgart have matched the engineers and produced a pair of bucket seats that must be the envy of all other sports car drivers. They grip, support, relax, and ventilate your body supremely well besides giving a splendid driving position.' *Autocar* liked the seats too: 'Careful matching of the seat upholstery to the suspension eliminates any springiness or tendency to bounce on the seat – essentially this is a car which you sit "in", not "on".'

Two Roofs

Operating either top on the W113 did not give the same satisfaction as the simple 'slow down and throw back' operation of its English and Italian contemporaries. Instead, they were both more complicated, but with a purpose.

There were a few more steps to removing either roof on a W113, but the rewards were watertight motoring with hoods attached and cleans lines with no top at all. The driver in these rather grainy images is Karl Kling.

UNFAIR COMPARISON

The end of the line at the Sindelfingen plant shows the little differences for each market, with a right-hand-drive car without side mirror, an Italian car with side marker lights, a French car with yellow headlights, and an American car with the different headlight arrangement.

Today, the SL 500 and the Jaguar XKR offer comfort for two (with occasional child use possible in the back seats in the Jag) and a similar 0–60mph performance. Both are available on the international market for about the same money. Back in 1963, their predecessors, the 230 SL and the E-Type, were still seen as competitors, but the playing field was not even.

In the export haven of the USA, a Series 1 1963 E-Type sold for $5,525. The 230 SL roadster debuted on the same market for $818 more. For that extra cash Mercedes buyers got a car that made 50 less horsepower and weighed 390lb (177kg) more. Like the Mercedes, the Jaguar was a capable sports car, but the 230 SL had the advantage of being much more comfortable. The real appeal of the Mercedes over the Jaguar came from the reliability of the three-pointed star badge. Unlike the E-Type, the 230 SL was viewed as prestigious everyday transport because it was engineered not only to start up every time, but also to offer a level of comfort from flawless items, such as a weather-tight hood.

So it would appear that maybe the Jaguar and Mercedes sports cars were not competitors? In fact, this end of the premium roadster and coupé market was so vast that the Jaguar and Mercedes were some of the closest opponents. It may seem a cliché to reference the 230 SL as a car in a class by itself, but it had no direct rival. The 230 SL undercut the speed and price of true exotic touring machines such as the Ferrari 250 GT, it offered more creature comforts than focused sports cars such as the Porsche 356, and the 230 SL carried a more modern image than other medium-volume sports cars, like the ageing Austin-Healey 3000.

So was the 230 SL a bespoke machine at a cut-rate price? Not quite. Two cars had a bit of a showdown at the International Motor Show at London's Earl's Court in 1963. Mercedes was giving Britain a taste of the new 230 SL, and Morgan was debuting its version of a modern car, the Plus Four Plus. Morgan's promotional material claimed that 'the enthusiast will find this the ideal sports car for tireless long-distance travelling'. Like its siblings, the Morgan had the 100bhp engine out of the Triumph TR4, but, with a sleek two-seater fibreglass body, it offered a top speed of 110mph (176km/h). The wheelbase was within a few inches of the 230 SL and the 0 to 60mph was only about a second behind the German. But the British coupé was hardly an SL fighter. It still carried the old-world construction and an ageing suspension. Morgan relied on the US market to sell these cars, and exported around 40 per cent of the Plus Four Plus production over the next 5 years – unfortunately, that was only ten cars. The first shipment of 230 SLs to reach the other side of the Atlantic was bigger than that, even if the Mercedes cost nearly twice as much in the USA.

There were other cars that came closer to the W113's price, but they brought a different attitude to the driveway. The 1963 Alfa Romeo 2600 Spider had 25 less horsepower and weighed 150lb (68kg) more than the 230 SL. This deficit may have been

Mercedes has the new 230 SL draw a crowd in front of the Stuttgart television tower.

small enough to put the two cars in the same league, but the Alfa's $4,995 base price meant that the 230 SL roadster represented a 27 per cent price hike. (Those who braved Alfa's dubious reputation for reliability and quality may be considering it a wise investment today as only 2,255 were ever produced.) Lancia's Flaminia coupé and spider had a similar price to the 230 SL in the USA, as well as comparable power and dimensions, but, like the Alfa, it was a passionate Italian machines more likely to be driven by a lothario.

Clearly, with the 230 SL, Mercedes had found a niche that had not previously been exploited. The car was nimble and spirited but some of its all-out sportiness had been traded for comfort. It was the sports car for grown-ups and the reliable second car for the millionaire playboy to drive when his exotic was once again at the garage. While speed had traditionally been the selling point of the roadster, Mercedes liked to tout in its advertising: 'The 230 SL is one of the world's most *solid* two-seaters.'

The 100lb (45.5kg) Pagoda roof could be freed by detaching locking latches located at the base of both rear quarter windows and then turning the two locking handles at the top of the windscreen. Mercedes recommended that the dealer was the best place to have this roof removed, but even they acknowledged in the instructions that two people could perform the operation.

The soft top was a little more complex to take down. This was done by operating a lever behind the left seat, to release the tonneau cover, and releasing the central locking pin for the rear part of the roof. The rear portion could then be folded upwards towards the windscreen, exposing the tonneau cover and allowing it to open, revealing the storage well. The front part of the roof was detached at the windscreen using locking handles that were similar to the ones on the coupé top. The front of the roof could then be raised and, as it and the folded rear portion were pushed backwards, the roof fell into the storage well. The tonneau cover could then be closed with the same precision as a Mercedes car door.

This operation was simple to understand, but it was a more complicated initial procedure than on other roadsters of its day. Unlike many of its peers, the 230 SL did not allow for the hood to be folded down without the driver leaving his seat. However, the W113 would prove its convenience when drivers of the other sports cars were eventually forced to get out and properly secure their folded hood behind a fabric tonneau cover. It was this element of the hood operation that led one magazine to refer to the 230 SL's process as 'the fastest soft-top in the world'.

The unconventional hood was a reflection of the 230 SL's quality. Not only did the 230 SL have the sleek appearance of a fully stored hood, but also the extra steps needed to secure the soft top of the W113 made it hold stable at speeds of around 90mph (145km/h). It was a continuation of the Mercedes tradition of weather-tight hoods for high-speed machines, demonstrated earlier on cars such as the 300 SL roadster.

The attention to detail meant that owners also had to be somewhat mindful of their soft tops. Although Mercedes was quite good at keeping water out of the car, there were elements that went beyond their control. As on other convertibles of the day, the fabric used for the hood could hold moisture or become deformed when compacted. Neither issue was a problem during short-term storage, but it did need to be taken into account. Mercedes specifically recommended that any customer who used the coupé top for an extended period of time should either have the soft

The hard top not only sealed out the weather but was also needed for the optional ski rack.

top removed at the dealership, or would need to remember to remove the coupé roof and raise the fabric top several times a year to vent the cloth hood.

Selling a New SL

Advertising the SLs was nothing new for Mercedes. In previous years the company had used the sporting character of the 300 SL and 190 SL to sell its cars, but marketing the 230 SL would be quite different. Alongside the established image of SL performance there would need to be more emphasis on the more luxurious elements of the car. This was very evident in the German promotional film that featured the company-sponsored racing driver Karl Kling demonstrating the build quality. It ended with Kling's committed endorsement: 'This is a car for driving individualists for whom sportiness without a comfortable ride and exclusivity without

worldwide service are simply not good enough. It is for those who expect one model to provide everything.'

Some of the first print advertisements were based on the idea of the car representing the 'best of all worlds'. One piece for the UK visually represented the metaphor of wearing multiple hats by showing a racing helmet alongside a bowler hat, to emphasize both the 230 SL's rally prowess (*see* Chapter 7) and its win at the European Concours d'Elégance in Heidelberg. Other ads would show the car in the background during upper-class leisure activities such as archery or horse-riding. The message was becoming clear. The 230 SL was here to define a certain lifestyle, not to deliver all-out speed.

The 230 SL also offered Mercedes a new opportunity to acknowledge the buying power of women. Where once women had merely been draped over the bonnet of a new car, the company recognized that it was time for a fresh perspective. A German-language advertisement appeared with a picture of a 1960s modern woman parallel parking her 230 SL

It used to fill men with pride to gallop across open country on one HP to the terror of evildoers and to the delight of pretty damsels in need of protection. - The horseman's era has passed but not man's delight in power, speed and rhythm. Our age offers new, greater opportunities. 1963 has one of particular appeal - a new sportscar of international rank, the 230 SL with the Three Pointed Star. This new Mercedes-Benz makes all the dreams it inspires come true. A few facts: 168 HP fuel injection engine with exceedingly lively response, disc brakes on front wheels, safety based on a sturdy chassis, comfort of a luxury sedan. The 230 SL is supplied as a roadster with soft top, a coupé with slender roof giving excellent visibility or a combination of the two, with both soft and hard tops. Power, quality and style, three distinctions combined in one car: the Mercedes-Benz 230 SL. For full information please mail the adjacent coupon. We shall be glad to be at your service

MERCEDES-BENZ

To: Export Division, Daimler-Benz AG, Stuttgart Untertuerkheim. Pleası send your illustrated literature describing all Mercedes-Benz models to

Rank and Name

Address

City

Phone Number
(in block letters, please)

Mercedes aiming the 230 SL at the gentleman driver.

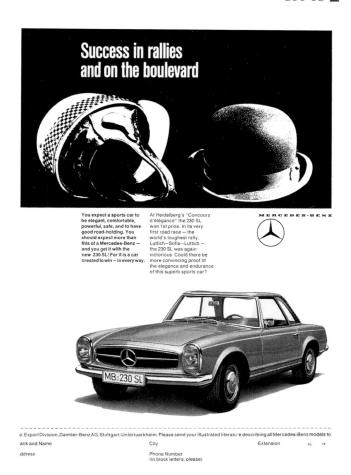

Success in rallies and on the boulevard

You expect a sports car to be elegant, comfortable, powerful, safe, and to have good road-holding. You should expect more than this of a Mercedes-Benz — and you get it with the new 230 SL! For it is a car created to win – in every way.

At Heidelberg's "Concours d'élégance" the 230 SL won 1st prize. In its very first road race -- the world's toughest rally, Luttich—Sofia—Luttich — the 230 SL was again victorious. Could there be more convincing proof of the elegance and endurance of this superb sports car?

MERCEDES-BENZ

o: Export Division, Daimler-Benz AG, Stuttgart-Untertuerkheim. Please send your illustrated literatu˙e describing all Mercedes-Benz models to

ank and Name   City   Extension

.ddress   Phone Number
                             (in block letters, please)

Advertisements often referred to rally and concours victories.

in a crowded urban area. The text was aimed at highlighting the comfort features available, such as the power steering and automatic transmission. Using a woman to demonstrate the luxury options of the car clearly came in a little short of total equality, but, for its era, it was a leap ahead to show her as a driver rather than just as an excited passenger.

The US market would pose one of the toughest advertising challenges for the W113. Mercedes executives had identified the USA as 'the largest export market for German-built cars', but it was a market that had always been a fickle in its automotive preferences. Mercedes had made inroads there – in 1966 the USA accounted for 6 per cent of Mercedes-Benz's annual sales – while still defying the country's conventional wisdom that a car should get lower, wider and longer with each passing year. As Mercedes was trying to dig further into the US market, at the same time maintaining its international appeal, the W113 was a bit caught in the middle. After

all, while Europeans were concerned about displacement for tax purposes, Americans were celebrating it. The Beach Boys were unlikely to follow up their song '409' (singing the praises of the 6.7-litre Chevrolet V8 engine) with a composition about the 140 cubic inches of the 230 SL!

On paper, a 230 SL did not seem like it should be worth its higher price, which was almost the equivalent of the average annual family income of $6,900. It was not a car with the supercar status or price of the 300 SL, so why did it command nearly a year's salary? Customers could buy a bigger, quicker and sometimes even rarer car for less money. The job of the Mercedes marketing executives was to sell that more tangible characteristic: engineering. They decided to tackle the topic head on by running full-page advertisements in the USA with the headline: 'Why the Mercedes-Benz 230 SL costs $6,343'.

The ad explained everything from build quality and rally victories to the virtues of its shiftable automatic transmission. It

Es macht Spaß,
einen Mercedes-Benz zu fahren

Sicherheit und Komfort sind für jeden einzelnen Mercedes-Benz selbstverständlich. Die Möglichkeit, den Komfort zu steigern, bieten Ihnen die Mercedes-Benz Sonderausstattungen. Hier nur ein Beispiel: die Daimler-Benz Servolenkung. Sie werden fragen, was eine Servolenkung ist und wie sie bewirkt; eine vom Motor angetriebene Öldruckpumpe, die Ihnen je nach Situation und Kraftaufwand die Arbeit beim Lenken abnimmt. Mit ihr wird das Rangieren und Parken zum Spiel. Auch für Damen. Von zwei Fingern ohne Kraftaufwand gelenkt, rollt der Wagen in die Parklücke. Bei jeder Fahrtsituation benötigen Sie die gleiche Kraft: beim Schnell- und Langsamfahren, beim Parken und z.B. bei einer kurvenreichen Paßfahrt. Und immer bleibt der gute Kontakt zur Fahrbahn erhalten.

Wenn Sie Ihren Mercedes-Benz nach eigenen Wünschen ausstatten wollen, steht Ihnen ein reichhaltiges Programm zur Verfügung. Unter anderem: Daimler-Benz Automatisches Getriebe, Stahl-Schiebedach, Kühlanlage, zahlreiche Sonderlackierungen, automatische Antenne, Spezial-Koffersatz für die Maße Ihres Kofferraums und vieles mehr.

Fragen Sie jemand, der einen Mercedes-Benz mit Servolenkung hat, oder machen Sie uns eine Probefahrt. Sie werden begeistert sein. Wir informieren Sie auch gern ausführlich über weitere Sonderausstattungen.

MERCEDES-BENZ
Ihr guter Stern auf allen Straßen

Mercedes advertisement making a genuine appeal to women.

The 7 loudest gripes against sports cars—and how the Mercedes-Benz 230SL squelches every one.

Mercedes explains to the US market how its negative perceptions about foreign sports cars do not apply to the 230 SL.

must have been successful, because not only was it continually updated as prices changed, but it was also revised and reused for future generations of the W113.

Another advertisement for the USA addressed the '7 loudest gripes against sports cars'. The majority of Americans viewed foreign sports cars as fun, but less reliable and with a harsher ride than the family saloon they might have been used to driving. The 230 SL came from a very different point of view, and Mercedes devoted nearly a full page of text to explain the principles. However, they were still at pains to point out that 'the 230 SL is not … a pantywaist'!

Outside Visions

Just because a design is a hit does not mean that others will not try to improve on it. In the 1960s, even the Jaguar E-Type,

which was considered by many to be the best-designed car around, was re-worked by Bertone to create the Espada-like Pirana. It should be no surprise, therefore, to learn that the 230 SL, a very German sports car in its understated elegance, would be treated to a little Italian flair.

Pininfarina

The first of these treatments came while the W113's design was still fresh. At the 1964 Paris Motor Show, Ferrari was showing off a 275 GTB from Pininfarina. But the Ferrari was not the only design that had been reworked by the Italian company. They had also recreated a 230 SL as a fixed coupé concept design.

From the front, the Pininfarina car looked like 230 SL, but something was slightly different. The elongated nose of this

A MERCEDES SL SALOON?

Mercedes W118 prototype.

Mercedes identified a need to compete in a smaller class of cars as early as the mid-1950s. It had just replaced the ageing 170 V with the 180 Ponton model, but Mercedes chief engineer Fritz Nallinger saw a gap for a smaller car that could be the 170 V's true successor. 'It is clear that the body must be new, with a smaller interior and smaller window areas compared with the W120', he said. 'Width and length will be like the 170 S, two-door body, bulkhead, dashboard, luggage compartment like the W120, front seats like the 170 V.'

A design study was begun in 1953, based on meeting these standards. Rather than adapt the Ponton's design for the smaller car, it was given the face of the sportier 190 SL. This project, known under the code W122, was nearly ready for production by the late 1950s, but by then its moment had passed at Mercedes. The W122 was based on Ponton parts, and engineers were already preparing that car's successor. Plus, Daimler-Benz had acquired Auto Union during this time, and any small Mercedes would directly compete with the largest DKWs.

W118 prototype interior.

A MERCEDES SL SALOON? *CONTINUED*

Mercedes would revisit the idea of an entry-level car at the dawn of the Pagoda age. Prototype W118 very much had the face of the contemporary modern SL. The focal point of the front was the large Mercedes tri-star emblem – a feature that had previously been reserved for the Sport Leicht cars only – hanging on a wide grille. The roof did not have the same inward slope as the contemporary SLs, but its flat appearance was reminiscent of a Pagoda. Even Mercedes would officially acknowledge the resemblance: 'With their SL face, low beltline, roof attachment clearance and rear design, the test vehicles produced were close to the Mercedes-Benz 230 SL (W113) in terms of style.'

Unlike the W122, the timing for the W118 entry-level car was beginning to look more promising at Mercedes. The company knew that the two-stroke motors used by their subsidiary Auto Union would not be popular for very long. Mercedes could keep the DKW factory in Ingolstadt busy with its small car and engine, which had now evolved into a high-compression 1.7-litre inline four-cylinder.

Ludwig Kraus, whose earlier work included the 300 SLR, was put in charge of this SL-like four-stroke saloon, and dispatched to the Auto Union headquarters to help with the planning. However, the climate soon changed at Mercedes, with the start of negotiations in 1964 for the sale of Auto Union to Volkswagen. Mercedes no longer had a factory at its disposal for the entry-level model. Instead, the work on the project would make way for the first post-Second World War Audi and help to give VW its first water-cooled engine.

Might the W118 have been an effective competitor for the BMW New Class (from the 1500 to the 2002)? It is impossible to do any more than speculate. But there is something more to this twice-tried concept. With enough of the Pagoda coupé/roadster design elements used in selling a more sensible saloon car, arguably the W118 could have been the grandfather to the modern Mercedes CLS as well as the Avantgarde trim on the C-Class.

The flat roofline helped give the W118 prototype the look of the 230 SL with the pagoda roof in place.

The clean lines of the rear share the structure of the W113 or the future Peugeot 204.

Tom Tjaarda with the Pininfarina 230 SL at Pebble Beach in 1997.

design still carried many of the basic lines of the production car but was it given a little more space to develop and the grille was given a more aggressive rake. The fixed coupé roof allowed the rear to have a more sporting design. The longer back glass gave it a less abrupt meeting with the boot, and the entire rear was able to be more sleek. In many ways, the Pininfarina 230 SL carried a posterior that brought it quite close to the Ferrari 330 GT.

In profile, the Pininfarina concept was unmistakably as crisp as the production 230 SL, but, where the original had straight sides, the Italian coupé's extra surface creases along the sides gave it a slightly more muscular look without being overly beefy. Looking at the two cars was something like comparing Sean Connery and Roger Moore filling out James Bond's white tuxedo.

Pininfarina has never been known for conservative design, so its version of the 230 SL was probably purposely made to have a clear resemblance to the production car. According to Tom Tjaarda, who penned this design at Pininfarina: 'The management at Pininfarina did have a sincere desire that the Mercedes management would be interested to participate in a limited production programme of this prototype/show car.'

This might have been the right partnership because the departure of the 300 SL left a hole in the Mercedes line-up. Part of the justification for the creation of the W113 was to make a performance car that was a bit more suitable for mass production than the 300 SL. Since the days of Emil Jellinek, Mercedes-Benz had offered sports cars that were accessible only to the highest and wealthiest echelons of society. The Pagoda cars could easily meet the needs of this clientele in terms of comfort but not necessarily in terms of exclusivity.

Pininfarina might have been a perfect partner to offer a low-volume Mercedes without interfering with the German company's plans to focus on expanding its manufacturing might. 'This was never to be', Tjaarda recalled. 'It also seemed that the Mercedes management really did not even want to discuss the matter and just let Pininfarina know that the matter was closed. End of story.'

This kind of tale can cause the imagination to run away with fantasizing about what might have happened if Mercedes-Benz had been more receptive to Batista Pininfarina. Mercedes was out of competition with Ferrari on the track, but what would have happened had they utilized its design house on the street? The market for a Mercedes with an Italian accent can only be a matter of speculation today, but, because the Pininfarina 230 SL coupé remained a bespoke creation, that car is the ultimate Pagoda collector's item.

According to Tjaarda, the car went through some changes after it disappeared from the show circuit. A few decades

The restored Pininfarina 230 SL won its class at the 1997 Pebble Beach Concours d'Elégance.

later the Pininfarina 230 SL coupé showed up at the Pebble Beach Concours d'Elégance, painted red and looking rather worn. It was not long after the car had ended up in the possession of a collector named Weston Hook. He restored the Pininfarina 230 SL to its original prototype condition, including the silver paint, and then brought it back to Pebble Beach in 1997, where it won its class.

The SLX Shooting Brake

Shortly after Pininfarina's car left the show circuit, another Italian design house gave its interpretation of what the W113 could be. Pietro Frua created a shooting-brake version of the 230 SL known as the SLX. Where the Pininfarina car was clearly a Pagoda SL infused with Italian DNA, the Frua creation had a different lineage.

In the front the headlights and fender mountings seemed to be the only pieces taken from the 230 SL. The chrome grille used on the contemporary saloons was installed, making the Frua car look more like the 300 SE coupé. The aluminium bonnet and front panels had to be modified to fit the new chrome work, which only enhanced its likeness to the larger cars.

From the side, the doorline and below was one of the few parts of the car that was pure W113. Above that the door

glass was squared off so that it could provide a transition into the rear hatch section. From the b-pillar rearwards the car resembled some of the Fura-designed BMW Glas hatchbacks. The rear carried the W113 bumpers and lights, but the hatch made the 230 SLX look like the future Mercedes W123 estate.

Amateur Efforts

Just because the established designers could not get an alternative body for the W113 into production, amateurs were not deterred from having a go at the car. One notable example came from a gentleman named Karl Schaller, who changed only three main pieces in order to create a look that was all his own. Schaller took a 230 SL and removed the pagoda roof as well as unbolting the standard bonnet and boot. The entire front end was covered with a new one-piece plastic unit that fitted over the unmodified fenders. Because the SL wore the new piece like a mask, it created an overhang for the entire front end. Much like the Frua design, the roof was modified to accept a rear hatch, but Schaller's car had a steeper rake that went all the way to the end of the car. These pieces were blended into the body by using the Pagoda's crease in the fender line as the seam for laying the new panels.

Overall, the car had a peculiar appearance. The extended frontal area over the headlights and the grille cast a long shadow over the car's face, and dark colours on flat panels were used to disguise the modifications in the rear. Schaller's W113 look a bit like the W114-based ESV (Experimental Safety Vehicle) #13, which actually debuted a year after the W113 left production. But where ESV 13 used function over style to absorb impacts better, Schaller's car was just considered an awkward design. Although Schaller had plans to produce his panels to transform Pagodas into shooting brakes, no car is known beyond Schaller's one prototype.

Changes Over the Years

Only first-year models of the 230 SL received a full-circle inner chrome ring on the steering wheel. Although this ring was a part of the 300 SL and 190 SL, Mercedes engineers finally realized that it interfered with the driver's view of the instruments. From February 1964 on, the chrome ring had the top half flattened, to help with an unobstructed view.

In November 1965 Mercedes worked to alleviate some of the complaints about the four-speed manual transmission. At this point, production of the 250 SE had begun, and the ratios for its standard transmission were utilized across the line-up,

The steering wheel was changed early in 230 SL production so that the chrome trim ring was no longer in the way of viewing the gauges.

End of the line – a 230 SL from 1967.

including the 300 SE and the 230 SL. The four-speed manual gearbox now had tighter ratios: 4.05 for first gear, 2.23 for second, 1.40 for third, and 1.0 for fourth.

Even after the gear ratios were changed, one of the main gripes about the 230 SL that came from spirited drivers was the fact that it still had the four-speed transmission. Enthusiasts felt that the power could be even smoother with an extra gear. Mercedes offered a fix for this by making a ZF manual five-speed transmission available from May 1966 onwards, paired with a 4.08:1 rear axle ratio. The result took 0–100km/h times from 11.1 seconds down to 9.7. There were few takers for this option, so, considering it is one of the rarest and quickest 230 SLs made, it has become quite a desirable collectable.

Another 230 SL that collectors might enjoy is one that is rare by birth. The 230 SL ended production in January 1967,

and only 185 examples were built that year, accounting for less than 1 per cent of total 230 SL production.

Impact

The Mercedes 230 SL had an interesting impact on the automotive world. There were plenty of elements Mercedes got right, such as the ease of operation and solid road feel, but there were also plenty of criticism for issues such as the soft suspension and low power for its price class (especially evident in the horsepower-driven US market). Despite the reservations, however, the 230 SL always seemed to be the one wearing the crown. Rarely had a car captured the heart of so many drivers, not because it was the most talented, but because it was the best all-round contender they had seen to date.

Fitted luggage was available from the outset.

230 SL OPTIONS AT LAUNCH

Item	Cost (DM)
Automatic radio antenna	180
(without radio installed)	210
Coupé roof (including chrome bars for ski rack)	1,100
(chrome bars for ski rack)	40 (not priced at launch)
'D' badge	8
Power steering	550
Fire extinguisher	60
Glare-free spotlights	50
Fitted luggage	365
1 large suitcase (95 DM)	
2 medium suitcases (80 DM)	
1 toiletry bag (75 DM)	
1 leather strap (35 DM)	
Leather interior	800
Rear transverse seat (MB-Tex)	200
Rear transverse seat (leather)	250
Radio – Becker Grand Prix	650
Radio – Becker Mexico	630
Radio – Becker Europa	490
Seatbelts (per seat)	55
First aid kit	30

Colour Combinations at Launch

Colour	Paint code	MB-Tex interior Colour	Leather interior Colour	Cloth hood Colour
White	050	turquoise	turquoise	black
		bronze	light bronze	black
		ecru	ecru	black
		dark blue	dark blue	marine blue
		red	red	black
		cognac	cognac	black or brown
White-Grey	158	bronze	bronze	black
		ecru	ecru	black
		red	red	black
		cognac	cognac	black or brown
Light Ivory	658	ecru	ecru	black or brown
		caviar	black	black

230 SL OPTIONS AT LAUNCH
CONTINUED

Colour Combinations at Launch *continued*

Colour	Paint code	MB-Tex interior Colour	Leather interior Colour	Cloth hood Colour
		red	red	black
		cognac	cognac	black or brown
Papyrus White	717	dark blue	dark blue	marine blue
		caviar	black	black
Light Beige	181	bronze	light bronze	brown
		ecru	ecru	brown
		caviar	black	black
		red	red	black
		light cognac	light cognac	black
Dark Blue	332	ecru	ecru	black
		red	red	black
		light grey	light grey	black
		white grey	white grey	black
		cognac	cognac	black
		light cream	light cream	black
Signal Red	568	ecru		
		caviar		
		white grey		
		light cream		
Dark Burgundy	573	ecru	ecru	black
		white grey	white grey	black
		light cream	light cream	black
Graphite Grey	190	ecru	ecru	black
		light grey	light grey	grey
		white grey	white grey	grey
		cream	light cream	black
Dark Green	268	ecru	ecru	black
		white grey	white grey	black
		cognac	cognac	black
		cream	cream	black

Colour Combinations at Launch continued

Colour	Paint code	MB-Tex interior Colour	Leather interior Colour	Cloth hood Colour
Black	040	turquoise	light turquoise	black
		ecru	ecru	black
		red	red	black
		light grey	light grey	black or brown
		white grey	white grey	black or brown
		cognac	cognac	black
		cream	cream	black

SEPTEMBER 1963

Colour	Paint code	MB-Tex interior Colour	Leather interior Colour	Cloth hood Colour
Light Ivory	670		medium blue	black
			dark green	black
			olive	black
Dark Auburn	460		light yellow antique	black
			auburn	black
			egg shell	black

Metallic Colours

Colour	Paint code	MB-Tex interior Colour	Leather interior Colour	Cloth hood Colour
Beige	462		red	brown
			light red	brown
			ecru	black
			auburn	brown
			olive	black
Silver Grey	180		blue	black
			medium blue	marine blue
			dark green	black
			green	black
			burgundy	black
Moss Green	834		light yellow antique	black
			brown	black
Blue	387		burgundy	black
			egg shell	black

TWO-TONE

Colour	Paint code	MB-Tex interior Colour	Leather interior Colour	Cloth hood Colour
White/Black	050/040	turquoise	turquoise	brown
			light red	brown

230 SL OPTIONS AT LAUNCH
CONTINUED

Colour Combinations at Launch continued

Colour	Paint code	MB-Tex interior Colour	Leather interior Colour	Cloth hood Colour
			auburn	black
			red	brown
			burgundy	brown
White/Dark Auburn	050/460		red	black
White/Dark Blue	050/332		middle blue	marine blue
White/Graphite Grey	050/190		anthracite grey	grey
White-Grey/Havana Brown	158/408	bronze	bronze	brown
			auburn	brown
			brown	brown
White-Grey/Graphite Grey	658/408		red	grey
			light red	grey
			anthracite grey	grey
Ivory/Havana Brown	658/408	ecru	ecru	brown
Papyrus White/Dark Blue	717/332		blue	black
Papyrus White/Dark Green	717/190		dark green	black
Papyrus White/Dark Burgundy	717/460		burgundy	black
Papyrus White/Graphite Grey	717/190		anthracite grey	grey
Light Beige/Dark Auburn	181/460	red	red	brown
			light red	brown
			auburn	brown
			brown	brown
Light Beige/Havana Brown	181/460		ecru	brown
			brown	brown
Dark Blue/Black	332/040	light grey	light grey	light grey
			egg shell	black

Colour Combinations at Launch continued

Colour	Paint code	MB-Tex interior Colour	Leather interior Colour	Cloth hood Colour
Dark Blue/Papyrus White	332/717	light grey	light grey	light grey
Signal Red/Black	568/040	white-grey	white-grey	black
			ecru	black
			light yellow antique	black
			egg shell	black
Signal Red/White-Grey	568/158	white-grey	white-grey	black
Dark Burgundy/Black	573/040	white-grey	white-grey	black
			ecru	black
			light yellow antique	black
			middle grey	black
			egg shell	black
			brown	black
Graphite Grey/Black	190/040	white-grey	white-grey	grey
Graphite Grey/White Grey	190/158	white-grey	white-grey	grey
Dark Green/Black	268/040	cognac	cognac	beige or black
			light yellow antique	black
			middle grey	black
			egg shell	black
Black/Light Beige	040/181	cream	cream	cream
Ivory/Black	679/040		red	black
			light red	black
			ecru	black
			auburn	black
Ivory/Dark Burgundy	670/460		red	black
Ivory/Havana Brown	670/408		ecru	brown

METALLIC TWO-TONE

Colour	Paint code	MB-Tex interior Colour	Leather interior Colour	Cloth hood Colour
Anthracite Grey/Black	172/040		red	black
			burgundy	black
			middle grey	black

230 SL OPTIONS AT LAUNCH
CONTINUED

Colour Combinations at Launch continued

Colour	Paint code	MB-Tex interior Colour	Leather interior Colour	Cloth hood Colour
Red/Black	571/040		ecru	black
			light yellow antique	black
			egg shell	black
Moss Green/Black	843/040		ecru	black
			egg shell	black
Translucent Red/Black	567/040		light yellow antique	black
			egg shell	black
Silver-Grey/Graphite Grey	180/190		anthracite grey	grey

230 SL

Steel unibody with aluminium doors, boot and bonnet

Engine

Name	M127 II (Type 127.981)
Block material	cast iron
Head material	aluminium
Cylinders	inline 6
Cooling	water
Bore and stroke	82 x 72.8mm
Capacity	2306cc
Valves	12v sohc
Compression ratio	9.3:1
Fuel system	manifold-injection, mechanically controlled, Bosch 6-plunger fuel injection
Max. power	150bhp @ 5,500rpm (DIN) 170bhp @5,600 (SAE)
Max. torque	145lb/ft @ 4,200rpm (DIN) 159lb/ft @4,500rpm (SAE)
Fuel capacity	65ltr (14.5gal), 82ltr (18gal) from 1966 on

| 230 SL CONTINUED |

Transmission

Gearbox Clutch Ratios	four-speed manual (1963–65) dry single-plate	four-speed manual (1965–67) dry single-plate	four-speed automatic fluid coupling	five-speed manual (Sep. 1965–) dry single-plate
1st	4.42	4.05	3.98	3.92
2nd	2.28	2.23	2.52	2.22
3rd	1.53	1.4	1.58	1.42
4th	1	1	1	1
5th	NA	NA	NA	0.85
Reverse	3.92	3.58	4.15	3.49
Final drive	3.75	3.75	3.75	4.08

Performance

Top speed	124mph/200km/h	124mph/200km/h	121mph/195km/h	124mph/200km/h
0–62mph (0–100km/h)	11.1 sec	11.1 sec	10.7 sec	9.7 sec

Suspension and Steering

Front	double wishbone, coil springs, torsion bar stabilizer
Rear	single-joint swing axle with compensating spring, coil springs
Steering	recirculating-ball (power optional)
Tyres	185 HR 14
Wheels	steel
Rim width	5 ½ J x 14 H

BRAKES

Type	hydraulic dual-circuit brake system with vacuum booster; disc front, drum rear
Size	10in front, 9.8in rear

Dimensions

Track			
front	58.5in 1,486mm	Overall width	69.3in, 1,760mm
rear	58.5in 1,487mm	Overall height	52in, 1,320mm
Wheelbase	94.5in, 2,400mm	Unladen weight	2,855lb, 1,295kg
Overall length	168.7in, 4,286mm		

CHAPTER SEVEN

W113 GOES RALLYING

The 1955 Le Mans catastrophe set the wheels in motion for Mercedes to stop building cars that were designed for the race track. Even without the world of Formula One and sports-car racing, a company known for its fortitude would not be content to rest on its laurels, and Mercedes turned its attention to new forms of competition.

In the early 1960s rally racing was something of a sport for gentlemen. There was honour in taking home a rally title, but the competition tended not to get heated to a frantic pace. For example, ace driver Tony Brooks used rallying to get away from the rigours of Formula 1 racing and had a little fun using an Austin FX3 taxi as his competition car for the 1961 Monte Carlo Rally. Perilous events such as the Mille Miglia were gone and specialists such as Lotus and Abarth were not yet building purpose-built high-speed rally

machines (homologation and Group B road-going super machines could not even be imagined yet). Instead, production cars that could be driven flat out without breaking were the rulers of the sport. This is the era when the 90bhp Volvo P544 ruled the sport because it was a Scandinavian tank.

Mercedes-Benz works driver Eugen Böhringer drove a 220 SE to win the overall European Rally Champion title in 1962. For 1963, he could not wait to get his hands on the 230 SL. Böhringer figured that the lighter weight and shorter wheelbase of the W113 car would give him much better manoeuvrability through the Alps for the summertime Spa–Sofia–Liège Rally. He had won the event in the previous year in the saloon, so the new sports car would be a welcome advantage. There was only one problem: the 230 SL did not yet exist.

Böhringer would find rally success in 220 SE and 300 SE saloon cars, but he wanted to try a Mercedes with a shorter wheelbase.

Despite having to share this stretch of road with a motorcycle, the 1963 Spa–Sofia–Liège Rally had already taken its toll on the Böhringer/Kaiser 230 SL.

Böhringer was already preparing for the 1963 season before the public saw the W113. He spoke to the Mercedes-Benz Board of Management member and Chief Engineer Fritz Nallinger about possibly arranging to get the company's still unofficial new sports car ready for the rally circuit. Nallinger, a racer earlier in his career, was receptive to this idea and encouraged Böhringer to approach the rest of the Mercedes board during the 230 SL's première at the Geneva Motor Show in March. Since Mercedes was still working to get the car into regular production, it took a bit of convincing to undertake a racing programme. Eventually, the board gave Böhringer its blessing to take its new car rallying.

Under the direction of Erich Waxenberger, the Mercedes testing department was given a red 230 SL that would be specifically configured for the upcoming Spa–Sofia–Liège. In the engine compartment the output was raised by 10 per cent to 165bhp, an oil cooler was added, a 4.56 rear axle

was installed, and the gearing on the manual transmission was revised. Two racing lights were attached to the front bumper, and one was mounted in place of the Mercedes insignia on the front grille. The team also had the ability to switch between 13in and 15in wheels, depending on road conditions.

Anyone purchasing a W113 could opt for the hard top and delete the fabric hood to create the coupé version, but Böhringer's 230 SL went one step further. While production cars could remove the coupé roof, for safety reasons the pagoda top was permanently affixed to the rally car. Some at Mercedes even thought of referring to this very special edition as a 'Böhringer Coupé'.

Klaus Kaiser partnered with Böhringer for the 1963 Spa–Sofia–Liège Rally. The four-day, 3,400-mile (5,400km) event ran in the last week of August 1963. There were 120 cars at the start, but only 20 crossed the finish line. The #39 Böhringer/Kaiser 230 SL was in first place.

ABOVE: **Erich Waxenberger behind the wheel of the 230 SL rally car replica in December 2011.**

1963 Spa–Sofia–Liège Rally.

Eugen Böhringer (centre) and Klaus Kaiser (left) after winning the 1963 Spa–Sofia–Liège Rally.

This victory did not go unnoticed at Mercedes-Benz and the rally car was on the company's stand for the 230 SL's German introduction at the 1963 Frankfurt Motor Show. The UK arm of Mercedes took out full-page advertisements touting the car's rally win in time to coincide with the 1963 Earl's Court Motor Show in the autumn. While the London show did not get the #39 car to display, they were happy to report the news that there would be a more pedestrian version of the winning car available to see at the Mercedes stand.

The Belgian rally was a good fit for solidifying the W113's image as a sports car. While the single-joint swing-axle rear end would not be available in time for the gullwing SL, the low-pivot unit, with its low centre of gravity, was a nearly bulletproof item by the time the W113 was ready to rally. The car had the magic 94.5in wheelbase of the 300 SL, which made it a great-handling car, but the suspension was much

softer than that of its speedy predecessor, so the ride was better over rough terrain. The free-revving 2.3-litre inline six-cylinder engine was the largest and most powerful unit that Mercedes had in production at the time, except for the 3.0-litre. That larger motor would take Mercedes to victory in other rallies – Böhringer took two titles at other 1963 rallies using a 300 SE – but the 230 SL had potential, and the Spa–Sofia–Liège event had proved it.

Mercedes revelled in the Spa–Sofia–Liège victory so much that they dragged out the same 230 SL again in 1964, to try and repeat its victory at the rally. Drivers Martin Braungart and Dieter Glemser were given the previous year's winning car (now wearing #19), while Böhringer and Kaiser were back for a second run, in another red 230 SL, #31.

For the 1964 race there was more of an eye towards weight savings on the hardy 230 SLs. The chrome bumpers

Prior to the 1964 Spa–Sofia–Liège Rally: (left to right) Martin Braungart, Dieter Glemser, Alfred Kling, Ewy Rosqvist, Manfred Schiek, Eugen Böhringer, Rolf Kreder and Klaus Kaiser.

were removed, as was the grille. A few more pounds were saved by the replacement of the side windows with sliding side curtains. While the diet may have been of benefit in the race, the modifications took the once-elegant cars and gave them an appearance that was purely form over function. The front aesthetics of the two racers were not improved by the five competition lights (some of which were knocked off during racing) and US-spec headlight mountings.

As in the previous year, the gruelling rally took its toll on plenty of vehicles, with only twenty-one of ninety-seven entrants finishing the event. One of the fallen included Braungart/Glemser's #19, which had to be retired after electrical problems. The vehicle that had won in the previous year unfortunately could not handle the punishment 2 years in a row.

Böhringer and Kaiser fared better than their teammates and had another good Spa–Sofia–Liège showing. Had it not been for problems such as a defective cable and an accident with a sheep, the team might well have repeated their 1963 victory. Instead, the #31 230 SL came in third place (second in its class), just 2 minutes behind the car in front of it. Although Böhringer did not win this year, he was still presented with a gold trophy by the event organizers in recognition of his succession of podium finishes in the punishing rally.

Braungart and Glemser would get another chance to take the 230 SL across a finish line as they drove the newer ex-Böhringer/Kaiser in the 1965 Acropolis Rally. Even following a major setback caused by a policeman sending them in the wrong direction, the team was able to finish a respectable

US-spec headlights for the 1964 Spa–Sofia–Liège Rally.

Böhringer and Kaiser at the finish line for third place in the 1964 Spa–Sofia–Liège.

fifth. By this time the world of rallying was changing for more powerful vehicles, and the Pagoda cars were retired from factory competition.

Like any other race cars of their day, the W113 rally cars were well used during their time in service. The Mercedes-Benz Classic Centre was certain that the 1963 winning 230 SL had been scrapped, and settled for a re-creation to put on display. This was the common belief for nearly five decades, until the ex-Böhringer #39 reappeared in 2013 at the Stuttgart Retro Classics show. It turned out that one of the most celebrated racing 230 SLs had been used for many years as a refurbished road-going car and had spent its retirement near the Mercedes headquarters in Stuttgart. It had been running around incognito under Mercedes-Benz's nose until the current owner decided to rediscover its history.

The car first came to light when it was bought by Dr York Seifert at the 2011 Stuttgart Retro Classics event.

34th Spa–Sofia–Liège Rally from 25 to 29 August 1964.

Eugen Böhringer celebrating his 90th birthday by driving a re-creation of his rally car in 2002.

Eugen Böhringer (1922–2013) celebrating his 90th birthday at the Mercedes Benz Museum SL Exhibition on 22 January 2012.

The previous owner had suspected that it was a rally car but could not confirm it. Seifert decided to do his own investigations and tracked down the ownership history all the way back to a Mercedes-Benz employee who bought the car from the company in 1965. The body numbers matched Böhringer's car, and Mercedes-Benz confirmed that the car was indeed the lost rally car. The owner has since returned the exterior to its 1963 form.

One more W113 racer mystery remains. Writer Gregor Grant, who was no stranger to driving in rally events, borrowed a 230 SL from Mercedes while he attended the 1964 German Grand Prix. He reported in a September issue of his *Autosport* magazine that the Pagoda on loan was given 'the full rally treatment'. He was never given the exact details of this car, but it was clearly a unique machine. 'It was fairly obvious that this particular car had been put together with loving care by Uhlenhault's men', wrote Grant. 'It certainly had more horsepower than the production machine, was, if anything, smoother, and ticked over around 700rpm like a sewing machine.'

Mercedes' only record of this SL relates to it being used as an exhibition vehicle. While Grant did not know the exact power figures, he specifically mentioned a rather interesting five-speed gearbox installed on the 230 SL. There were other signs that this car had been in a very specific service to Mercedes-Benz. 'The car used was tastefully finished in green, but would not take any concours prizes, as there was a series of mysterious holes bored on the rear wings and on the bonnet – possibly a souvenir of past rallies', Grant deduced.

The 0–60mph run was reported at 10.8 seconds, which is slightly better than what could be accomplished when shifting the 230 SL with its normal four-speed automatic transmission. But the standard car would not be able to keep up for long up to 100mph, which Grant's SL hit in 23.4 seconds – about 12 seconds faster than the production automatic 230 SL. Grant also got his car up to a top speed of about 130mph, 5mph and 9mph more than the four-speed manual and automatic cars, respectively.

What made this car especially unique was that it was a right-hand-drive. Both of the two cars entered in the Spa–Sofia–Liège and Acropolis rallies were left-hand drive, so where did this one come from and what did it accomplish? The W113 *was* used at other events such as the Tour de France in 1964

Claude Picasso used his 1963 230 SL to drive the 28,000km Around the World in 80 Days Rally in 2000.

and the London–Sydney Marathon in 1969, but those sorts of entries were private ones. The mystery is still not solved.

The Pagoda SLs did not have factory support in rallying after the mid-1960s. The 1965 season began with new homologation rules that brought in low-volume near-prototype machines, so keeping pace for an overall victory would be near-impossible with these specialist machines. In addition, the 2.8-litre model showed up in the saloons first, and by the time it became available in the W113, there were already V8s available in the saloons. As a result, at the times when a production car was needed for a rally, the larger displacements would overshadow the Pagodas.

Although the W113s were out of favour for rallying, it did not matter for very long. The larger-displacement cars were not flattering when the first oil crisis hit in the 1970s and factory-backed entries would soon disappear. This left the

door open for private teams to work on development and out of this came the creation of AMG (Aufrecht Melcher Großaspach), the brainchild of former Daimler-Benz employees Hans-Werner Aufrecht and Erhard Melcher.

By the end of the 1970s Mercedes was re-entering the world of rallying. The SLs would play a dominant role, but this time it was the W113 successor. Four 450 SLCs entered the 1978 Vuelta a la América del Sur rally in South America. After 18,000 miles (28800km) of driving, two of the V8 SL coupés took the top two overall victory spots. A 5.0-litre version of the 450 SLC dominated the podium at the 1979 Bandama Rally in Africa and took the overall top spot again in 1980.

Although the SLCs had chalked up an impressive number of rallying victories, Mercedes' days in this competition were numbered. The changes that had come about when the W113 fell out of favour were leading to the creation of outrageous

Winners of the 1979 Bandama Rally (left to right): Björn Waldegård (2nd place), Hannu Mikkola (1st place), Andrew Cowan (3rd place). Mercedes-Benz 450 SLC 5.0 with trophies on the bonnet.

The W113 is a favourite for historic events such as the Bahamas Speed Week Revival.

machines that would eventually turn into the insanely quick but potentially lethal Group B cars. Mercedes was not going to be part of this era. In December 1980, the company pulled out of factory-backed programmes. Werner Breitschwerdt, then Daimler-Benz AG Board of Management spokesman for Development and Research explained: 'We have decided to put all our research resources and capacity into meeting our responsibilities for environmental protection.'

Today, the characteristics that made the W113s less than perfect for new car rallies have become a bit of an advantage.

Plenty of historic rallying (outside of serious competition such as FIA) sets a more manageable pace. An ideal car is one that is sporting, durable and comfortable. Not only does that fit the personality of the W113 well, but also the number of parts shared across the Mercedes line means that preparing and repairing these cars can be reasonably affordable. While it is by no means cheap to have a car equipped for this type of event, the W113 is more economical than many others. As historic rally events try to recapture the era of the gentleman's sport, the Pagoda cars are proving to be the perfect chaps.

CHAPTER EIGHT

W113 AND THE USA

The USA has always been a key market for the SLs, and the W113 was exactly the right car for the era in that country. The added production figures of the Pagodas did more than just fill a desire to export across the Atlantic – they were a necessary part of the rapid success story. The car and the country were built on an intertwined dependence that deserves to be fully explained.

Working the US Market

By 1965, Mercedes-Benz was exporting nearly half of its total production, and the USA was its most important foreign market. The W113 was setting new sales records in the USA, not only because this was the right car to sell, but also because the timing was right.

Max Hoffman was the man who opened the doors for many European companies wanting to sell cars in the USA. He knew that part of the key to import success in his market lay in sports cars and open-top motoring. That is why his influence was key to turning the 300 SL into a roadster and in the creation of the 190 SL.

Mercedes was one of the first German companies to reopen exports to the USA after the Second World War. When Hoffman began distributing Mercedes cars in 1952, there were only 36 Mercedes-Benz cars registered in the country. Hoffman was certain that the best way to re-establish the tri-star in the USA was to get the cars into the hands of celebrities and socialites. His interest was in the selling of cars, but as a distributor, he was less focused on offering the level of after-sales service that had helped to build the Mercedes-Benz reputation elsewhere. By 1957,

Hoffman showroom in Chicago (1955), representing multiple import brands in the USA.

when the Hoffman-encouraged 300 SL roadster was debuting, Mercedes sales had outgrown Hoffman's distribution scales. The image was suffering as parts were not available, and Mercedes began to search for a new partner.

In 1958, Mercedes thought they had found a better fit with the Studebaker Corporation. Mercedes cars would be sold through this established dealer network as part of a bigger deal with the managing parent Curtiss-Wright Corporation, which would allow Daimler-Benz to share its commercial vehicles and engines too, all within one conglomerate. Mercedes-Benz Sales was established in the USA as a subsidiary of the Studebaker Corporation.

Initially, this arrangement worked well for both companies. The benefit for Mercedes was that it took its cars out of showrooms that featured multiple imported brands, often their direct competitors. Now the manufacturer had access to a new dealer network that featured not only the workman brand of Studebaker, but also the American premium marque of Packard.

The advantage for the fledgling Studebaker-Packard was that Mercedes provided a much-needed extra revenue stream. Large companies were beginning to dominate the US car-manufacturing landscape – General Motors, Ford and Chrysler had quickly become known as 'The Big Three'

Paul O'Shea, sports-car director of the Studebaker-Packard, gets lassoed by Sandra Joan Meek, the Rodeo Queen of Las Vegas, during a 1958 Mercedes-Benz North America meeting. At the time Studebaker-Packard was in charge of Mercedes car distribution in the USA, and O'Shea was an accomplished racer in the 300 SL.

during this period. Studebaker-Packard hoped that the added distribution and sales traffic from Mercedes cars would help to keep it afloat.

During this agreement Mercedes products were added to over 400 Studebaker dealers across the USA. This could have been seen as a good measure, considering the 230 SL was designed to be a larger-volume car than the 300 SL. The problem was an over-saturation of the market. Heinz Hoppe was Mercedes-Benz's executive representative in North America, but he had not yet become the president for that market at the time of the Studebaker deal. In his autobiography *Serving the Star Around the World*, he described the problem: 'In Chicago, there were more MB than Cadillac dealers at the time, although the American market was selling ten times more cars in that city.'

Cracks in the Studebaker agreement rapidly began to appear. Service was still a problem because the large-volume Studebaker service departments did not have much practice working on the lower-volume Mercedes cars. Neither was sales a strong suit, as the same staff that sold Studebakers were now also trying to sell Mercedes products at significantly higher price. Hoppe reported the main reason given by one Studebaker dealer for having the foreign products on his lot: 'I'll never sell a Mercedes here unless some half-wit comes along and wants one, but I'll leave the star up on the building, because it raises my status in the area.'

By 1964 the scale of the inequality was beginning to be too much. Packard did not survive the recession of the late 1950s, and Studebaker was winding down its production. News was much more positive at Mercedes, which had sold nearly 100,000 cars in the USA since its return. It was time for Mercedes to be completely on its own. In March 1965, Mercedes-Benz of North America, Inc. (MBNA) opened its doors in the New York City suburb of Fort Lee, New Jersey. It was the company's first wholly owned sales organization outside Germany.

All but one of the 250 SLs visible in this picture were sent to the USA.

As the Pagodas were leaving production, Mercedes-Benz North America opened a purpose-built headquarters in Montvale, New Jersey.

When Mercedes ended its contract with Studebaker, all the dealer agreements were cancelled. Many of the dealers recognized, however, that Studebaker was a sinking ship, and Mercedes-Benz was able to re-sign 198 of the 318 that were in the former organization. (In its first year, MBNA had 231 franchises in total.) This is not the first time a foreign automaker has retained many of its dealers after venturing on its own. What was unique for Mercedes is that many of these dealers were long established in their territories with Studebaker and Packard products, and now Mercedes were serving as the flagship vehicles. This created one of the strongest customer bases possible for a foreign car company operating independently on US soil.

At the time when MBNA was formed, the W113 was still a relatively new product on the market. Under the new sales organization, it was a powerful tool to attract customers into the enhanced Mercedes showrooms. The 230 SL did not ride as harsh as the 300 SL, and it was more powerful than the 190 SL. This gave the car a nice appeal for the US market, possibly even for those customers who were ready to trade in their Studebaker Hawk GTs or Avantis (although these were not exactly equal swaps, considering that the 230 SL attracted a premium over the Avanti of about $2,200, or 50 per cent).

Despite the price, the Pagoda SL was the right sports car for Mercedes to have in its line-up as it was beginning to expand into the US market on its own. A car like the 300 SL was built in too few numbers and would have been spread too thinly across the dealer network, while the 190 SL was not powerful enough to be the flagship sports car of a premium brand. The 230 SL had the right mix of availability and prestige to present the exact image that the company wanted to re-establish across the USA. The mid-1960s was a perfect storm for Mercedes, in which a new product and a strong dealership body helped sales to jump in the era of the 230 SL, from 11,296 cars in 1964 to 20,691 in 1967 in the USA.

The Safety Revolution

The era of the 230/250 SL came at the beginning of a safety regulation avalanche in the USA, which would spread to most other markets across the globe. But why did the United States need so many regulations?

After the Second World War, the major US car manufacturers were not keen on selling safety. It was felt that the public did not like being reminded of the fact that cars could be dangerous; whenever the car companies did market safety features, it did not benefit sales. However, by the time of the W113, auto safety was becoming too big a concern to ignore. Traffic accidents in the USA were increasing at an alarming rate in the 1960s. According to *Time* magazine traffic fatalities jumped by 30 per cent from 1961 to 1966, while during the same period total vehicle registrations went up by about 22 per cent. 'The toll of Americans killed … since the introduction of the automobile is truly unbelievable', President Lyndon Johnson told the US Congress in 1966. 'It is at 1.5 million – more than all combat deaths suffered in all our wars.'

Some of this was a product of a particular culture. In that same speech, President Johnson also acknowledged that the USA was the only major nation that primarily relied upon privately owned and operated transportation. A new interstate highway system would take drivers across the USA on long car journeys that would be reserved for trains in many other countries. These endlessly straight roads required so little driver attention that they could induce a trance-like state, which was now being called 'highway hypnosis'. But the solution was not just better driver training.

Cars in the USA were heavy, traditionally built predominantly out of hard steel, and they did not necessarily fare well in an accident. Furthermore, aside from a few examples, American cars were built for style over function. Performer Sammy Davis, Jr. lost an eye in a 1954 car accident because Cadillac thought it would be chic to have a hard pointed cone as the centrepiece of the steering wheel. A

study determined in 1966 that, without intervention on the safety front, the USA was on a crash course to having one out of every two citizens injured in some way from an automobile accident.

It was time for things to change. The Chevrolet Camaro was introduced in late 1966, incorporating items such as a safety steering column and crumple zones. These features were revolutionary for the US manufacturers, but had been available on Mercedes-Benz vehicles for over six years. In fact, Mercedes was seen as a leader on the US market for safety.

A 1966 American study into the future of safer vehicles looked across the Atlantic for inspiration. It noted that 'Mercedes-Benz and Rover feature disc brakes on front wheels, while selected American cars show them as an option on some models', adding that 'the suspension system of the Rover and Mercedes-Benz assures better ride and cornering than is achieved in most American cars, and the crushable front ends of the Rover and Mercedes-Benz are promised by Ford for the '69 models'. It was not just the exterior that was safer, according to the study: 'Mercedes-Benz is further ahead in safety with protruding ends of all dash and door panel controls made of soft elastomers. The window operating mechanisms on manually operated windows are all well forward of the impact area of seatbelted passengers, and of the driver.'

Mercedes carried out extensive safety testing across its line-up.

The safety innovations and crash testing that went into developing the W113 meant that it already met or even exceeded the standards required by the USA later in the Pagoda's life.

Just because Mercedes-Benz cars were being championed as innovative did not excuse them from eventually having to adapt.

European Delivery Programme

Much of America's love for the roadster was rooted in post-Second World War society. Soldiers returned from Europe with a taste for nimble drop-tops, and some even went so far as to bring examples back with them. This prompted a few US car manufacturers to try their hand at European-inspired sports cars. The home-grown Chevrolet Corvette

and the British-American-Italian collaborated Nash-Healey were among the first, but these early cars, as well as the first few imports off the boat, failed to capture the imagination of the US market. It just was not the same experience without the challenging roads and ancient landscapes that had helped the Americans fall in love with such cars while they were abroad. So, rather than over-inject the European feel to their drivers, car companies such as Mercedes-Benz decided to bring their drivers to Europe.

In an initiative known today as the European Delivery Programme (EDP), Mercedes would allow owners to pick up their new cars directly from the factory. Participants

Mercedes-Benz changes the 230 SL to the 250 SL and continues its overseas purchase plan.

Progress can't be held back. The much lauded Mercedes-Benz 230 SL sports car has gained a 2.5-liter engine — and 4-wheel disc brakes to match the extra power. As before, members of the Armed Forces serving overseas can arrange purchase through a plan set up by the Daimler-Benz AG. Paying only U.S. $ 5,445.-* savings amount to hundreds of dollars compared to U.S. prices, and there is no red tape.

The Mercedes - Benz 250 SL was recently introduced to the public. You can order yours now. Pick up your 250 SL at the factory in Sindelfingen near Stuttgart, drive it during your overseas tour of duty, then take it home when you return. It's as easy as buying a car back home, too: clip the coupon for all the details on this remarkable car and the money-saving purchase plan.

A brilliant machine

You'll enjoy the pleasure of owning one of the world's superb sports cars, made even better by fitting of its larger 2.5-liter 6-cylinder engine and 4-wheel disc brakes (Some might say the 250 SL didn't really need its new 4-wheel disc brakes: the 230 SL — with discs in front and drums at the rear — already held Road & Track magazine's record for

The hardtop roof is concave, like a pagoda's. An ingenious engineering idea to increase visibility. A conversation piece, too.

fast stopping time. But Mercedes-Benz added just that much more stopping safety.) The 250 SL's top speed matches that of the 230 SL at 124 m.p.h. But added torque means quicker take-off and passing power.

Well enough left alone

The 250 SL keeps the same fully-independent suspension, rigid "unit" body and sheer handling genius of the 230 SL. As Autocar magazine states "the car can even be cornered hard enough for the tires to howl in pouring rain".

Unparalleled comfort

As before, the 250 SL provides luxurious comfort for two. In fact, the 250 SL has more legroom than a certain Rolls-Royce. The bucket-type seats (each measuring 23 inches in width) are designed and formed to properly support your body, eliminating fatigue.

Even in convertible form, the car is virtually sealed off from wind-blasts and draughts. Separate controls ensure complete heating and ventilation services for individual comfort. And noise -- that bane of life in so many sports cars -- is so muted inside this car that you and your passenger can talk in a normal tone of voice. No shouting.

Options

Power-assisted steering and a remarkable, 4-speed automatic transmission are two of the popular extra-cost options.

There are 3 models to choose from: the Roadster, with convertible top; the Coupe with a steel hardtop (as an optional extra for the Coupe only, you can order a rear bench seat), and the Roadster/Coupe, which offers both tops.

Clip the coupon now

For more facts on the 250 SL and other Mercedes-Benz models, plus complete details on military personnel purchase, clip and send the coupon below. It could be the shrewdest business transaction you have ever made.

MERCEDES-BENZ

* Price for the roadster model in standard execution and delivery at Daimler-Benz AG Sindelfingen factory near Stuttgart. Prices and specifications subject to change without notice. The U.S. equipment is available as an extra-cost option.

Mercedes-Benz motor cars and parts are distributed in the U.S. by Mercedes-Benz of North America, Inc., Fort Lee, N.J., U.S.A., a wholly owned subsidiary of Daimler-Benz AG, Germany.

To: Daimler-Benz AG · Export Division 4 · 7000 Stuttgart-Unterteurkheim · Germany

Please send your illustrated literature describing all Mercedes-Benz models to:

Rank and Name:
(in block letters, please)

Address: City:

Tourist pricing was also offered to US Armed Forces members stationed in West Germany. Advertisements reminded US military personnel that they could pick a car up at Sindelfingen, drive it during their overseas tour of duty, and then ship it when they returned home.

would arrive at Sindelfingen, tour the plant that produced their car, eat lunch on premises, tour the Mercedes Museum, receive the keys to their new car, and then be sent on their way to enjoy the European roads. Mercedes would take care of insurance for the time in Europe, and they would also include international customs licence plates that were valid throughout the continent. Those who did not want to pick up their cars in Germany could still participate in the EDP. For example, for an extra $216 Mercedes would hand over the keys to a US-spec 230 SL to its new owners in London.

When the customer's holiday was over, he or she would go home, and the car would be shipped to the USA. Owners

FOR SALE: 1967 230SL roadster, automatic transmission, red with brown interior, only 29,000 miles. Michelin tires like new. Reason for selling—going to Europe to buy another one. Asking $5000.00. Call Fort Wayne, Indiana, AC 219 637-███.

Classified ad from a 1969 edition of a Mercedes-Benz club newsletter.

did not even have to return to Stuttgart as Mercedes had arrangements through most major European cities.

The real benefit of purchasing a car from the European Delivery Programme was that the cars were sold at 'tourist' prices. This separate price list offered deep discounts on all Mercedes-Benz cars. The idea of picking a car up from the factory for a discount was not exclusive to US customers, but the discounts for Americans were exceptional. For example, in 1968 a 250 saloon could be purchased for $3,717, representing a 27 per cent discount on its retail price in the USA. Possibly one of the biggest discounts was the whopping 38 per cent offered on the seven-passenger 'Grand Mercedes' 600 limousine, which could be had for $16,408.

Not only did European Delivery give a break on price, it also created a tax advantage. At the time, the USA had lighter restrictions than other countries on how they taxed imported vehicles. Countries such as the UK required a certain mileage minimum and/or registered time on the road for an imported car to qualify for 'used' status. Cars that were sent to the USA, on the other hand, were eligible for the lower used-car tax rate almost immediately after European pick-up.

There were still some drawbacks to the programme. The tourist prices did not include shipping costs back to the USA and owners sometimes had to pay extra for US-specific parts that were already included on cars at local dealerships. Still, even after these expenses, there were genuine savings to be had. In its EDP literature, Mercedes used the example of a well-optioned 250 S to demonstrate that, even after all extra fees, including licensing and insurance while abroad, the plan would save the buyer $1,103 or 17 per cent.

Unfortunately, the prices were not quite as favourable for the W113. The tourist pricing on the Pagoda cars was as follows: in 1964, 230 SL Roadster $5,175, 230 SL Coupé $5,263, 230 SL Roadster/Coupé $5,451; in 1967, 250 SL Roadster $5,448, 250 SL Coupé $5,549, 250 SL Roadster/Coupé $5,745; in 1968, 280 SL Roadster $5,607, 280 SL Coupé $5,703, 280 SL Roadster/ Coupé $5,890. This represented

Customer picks up a US-spec Pagoda at the delivery centre in Sindelfingen.

around a 17 per cent discount off the US retail prices, but much of that would be eaten away after fees were applied. The average discount before costs on other cars in the Mercedes line came in at around 30 per cent.

A US customer who wanted to pick up a Pagoda in Stuttgart would have to factor in air travel, accommodation, overseas insurance and import tax before deciding not to use a local dealer. On the other hand, those who wanted a European getaway and also wanted to pick up their

Mercedes at the same time could count every day with their new W113 as a savings from rental car fees.

Today, the programme is still offered by most major manufacturers in Europe. Mercedes programme is now more comprehensive, providing such items as free accommodation for the first night near the factory and a travel concierge for the rest of the trip. Unfortunately, the pricing is now more uniform, with a flat 7 per cent discount on eligible vehicles.

CHAPTER NINE

250 SL

250 SLs on the Mercedes-Benz test track in Untertürkheim.

Mercedes knew that the W113 needed to have brisk performance. That was seen from the outset as the 220 SE's 2.2-litre six-cylinder motor was enlarged to 2.3 litres before the W113 hit the market. The engines were built to be driven hard, and it was at the upper rpm ranges where drivers found the best performance. Unfortunately, most owners don't have an open road to go play everyday, and needed to use their SLs in low-speed, urban situations. In such situations, the 230 SL could leave drivers wanting. This was especially true of the automatic transmission version, which comprised 40 per cent of all 230 SLs.

The 230 SL was by no means underpowered but, as larger engines came into the Mercedes family, the buying public began to wonder why the company's sports car did not change with the times. As a premium brand, with customers paying premium prices, Mercedes was in a bit of a bind. With its heavy reliance on the power-driven US market, the

limitations of the 2.3-litre engine were causing a problem. It was best summed up by the American magazine *Sports Car Graphic*: 'Mercedes has been aware of this weakness for several years – it has existed throughout several models – but it has been relatively reluctant to do anything about it because of the tax and economy advantages of the smaller engine size in the "World Market".'

Because US vehicle taxes and insurance were not closely related to engine size, the American public was having trouble understanding why Mercedes was not allowing its larger engines under the bonnet of the W113. 'Ever since the 250 series was introduced it seemed to us that the Mercedes-Benz 230 SL could benefit greatly from the substitution of the 250's 2.5-litre engine,' said *Road & Track*. 'Though the 230 SL was a model of roadholding, ride and structural integrity, its least pleasant feature was an engine that was neither quiet, smooth nor particularly powerful.'

Finishing the assembly line at Sindelfingen.

In 1966, the W113 reached its fourth model-year, and Mercedes knew it was time for a change. By November the first pilot run of 250 SLs were coming down the assembly line at Sindelfingen, and consumer cars would be online before the end of the year. The 250 SL was able to enter the W113's assembly line with great ease, because, aside from the engine, most major production pieces were a direct carry-over. Everything from the body panels to the carpeting was the same in the 250 SL as in the outgoing 230 SL.

The world got its first glimpse of the improved W113 at the Geneva Auto Show in March 1967, and the car made its US debut at the New York Auto Show in April. Still, the US and the UK did not receive any examples of the 250 SL until late spring – but for different reasons.

It took longer for cars to go from the end of the assembly line in Sindelfingen to the roads of the USA than it took them to reach the UK. As a result, US-bound 250 SLs were started well before the right-hand drive models destined for the UK, but they arrived at the dealerships at around the same time. The exception to this would be for anyone who had enough clout to persuade the factory to run a special order for him. One perfect example of this was Mercedes-Benz ace British driver Stirling Moss. He had been so impressed with the W113 that he had written a letter to

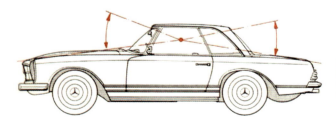

Das neuartige Flachdach mit seinen hochgezogenen Dachkanten ermöglicht einen außergewöhnlich großen Sichtwinkel nach oben und in alle Richtungen.

Drawing from the Mercedes-Benz catalogue touting the benefits to the driver of the pagoda-style roof.

Alfred Neubauer: 'In the many years I have been driving, I cannot remember wanting to own any car I have ever driven (with the exception of racing cars!) as much as this one.' Moss was very keen to get hold of an early 250 SL, but the factory had only begun producing left-hand-drive machines to send across the Atlantic. Still, Mercedes saw fit to send one UK-spec car down the line for its British Grand Prix and Mille Miglia winner. (Although this was a grand gesture of appreciation, it will be noted later how it was probably not too difficult to create this car.)

Moving From 2.3 to 2.5

The long-awaited extra grunt that a larger engine would provide in the SL did not come in the form of horsepower. The 250 SE's 2.5-litre six-cylinder engine (M 129) made the same 150bhp (170 SAE) as the 2.3-litre (M 127). The difference was the torque. The 250 SL's 159lb/ft @ 4,200rpm (173lb/ft @ 4,500 SAE) represented a 10 per cent increase over the 230 SL.

Torque is not as glamorous as horsepower in the world of sports cars, but the 250 SL was developed to address a specific problem. Automatic versions represented a sizeable proportion of the W113 sales, and the figures were growing. Drivers of these vehicles were more likely to set the trans-

mission in '4' (in other words, 'drive') and go about their journey without moving the gear lever again until it was time to park. Because this selection rarely utilized first gear the 230 SL could feel somewhat sluggish when setting off, as its engine was built to be run hard and develop more torque at higher rpms. The 2.5-litre was designed to work more harmoniously with the Mercedes four-speed automatic, by offering more grunt at lower engine speeds.

This is why at the launch of the 250 SL, Artur Keser, Head of Press for Mercedes-Benz in 1967, specifically claimed that the car could handle city traffic with much greater ease. This was due to the 2.5-litre providing 'an enormously increased tractive force even in lower speed ranges'.

The extra torque also had a positive impact on the performance. Mercedes listed the 250 SL's 0 to 100km/h figures as 10 seconds in the four-speed manual and 10.6 seconds for the four-speed automatic. This was an improvement of 1.1 and 0.1 seconds respectively. The optional five-speed manual stayed the same, at 9.7 seconds.

Reviewers writing for magazines and individual drivers often achieved better figures because, not only did Mercedes measure performance with two occupants in the car, but also the 250 SL was often quicker in Europe where a lower final drive ratio was optional (*see later*). For example, when *Car and Driver* performed its first test of the 250 SL, in August 1967, it recorded a 0 to 60mph time of 9.5 seconds.

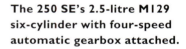

The 250 SE's 2.5-litre M129 six-cylinder with four-speed automatic gearbox attached.

OPPOSITE TOP: **A trailer hitch rated at 2,645lb (1,200kg) first appeared on the option sheet in February 1965. The added torque of the 250 SL must have been a welcome addition for those who would tow with their Pagodas.**

The performance was not the only reason for the upgraded engine. The 2.5-litre had a compression ratio of 9.5:1 and new oil-water heat exchanger for cooling. Possibly the most significant piece was the seven-bearing crankshaft, up from four in the 230 SL. Horsepower still peaked at 5,500rpm, with the red line at 6,500, but now the engine ran up to these tolerances much more quietly and smoothly.

California Coupé

The 250 SL's most significant change outside of the engine compartment was a new body option, nicknamed the California Coupé. As a variation on the coupé body style, the California Coupé removed the tonneau cover and storage well so that a folding rear bench seat could be installed. Although this was the first time the W113 could be advertised

The California Coupé offered luggage space that rivalled that of the boot when the seats were folded.

The California Coupé did not offer enough legroom to make the W113 a comfortable vehicle for four adults.

BOTTOM: **The California Coupé was weather-tight with the hard top in place.**

as a 2+2 grand touring car, the rear seat was quite cramped for any adult. Instead, most owners found that the best use for the extra space was to fold the bench flat, creating more storage space.

Naming this model after the US state known for sunshine and low rainfall was a not-so-subtle reminder that, because it had no room for a folding hood, it was not a good idea to get caught too far from home with the top off. Despite its limitations, however, the variation did not come cheap – it was a DM 510 option (or DM 640 to have the bench in leather).

This lack of versatility and useability made the California option one of the least popular W113s on the collector market. The roadster, convertible and standard coupé models were all interchangeable on the W113. A standard coupé could easily be transformed into a convertible with a soft top readily available from Mercedes-Benz or an aftermarket company. Unfortunately, the modifications required on the California Coupé in order to fit the rear bench removed the ability to add a canvas hood at a later date.

The good news is that the California Coupé should be one of the more affordable ways to purchase a W113. Just

250 SL UNFAIR COMPETITION

Reading reviews of the W113 cars when they were new can be a bit puzzling. They were expensive but not exotic, and quick but never fast. Yet they were still always good cars, in a class by themselves. They were more exclusive than the assembly-line clones, but the power and production figures kept them out of truly exotic status. So, while they had no real equal, it is interesting to explore some of the other options that were around when the 250 SL was introduced, in 1967. The UK was not the most important export market for the Pagoda cars, but, with a high concentration of domestic low-batch consumer-priced sports cars, it was a battleground worth conquering.

Triumph was experiencing a strikingly similar 1967 to Mercedes when it came to sports roadsters. Like the 250 SL, Triumph's new car featured a fuel-injected 2.5-litre engine in a familiar body. With its top speed of 125mph (200km/h), the new TR5 was so far almost a dead ringer for the 250 SL. Both cars had independent rear suspensions (although the set-up on the TR5 was more modern than the 250's swing axle), disc brakes (front only on the Triumph), and an optional hard top. And the TR5 was available for a very limited time (13 months) before a replacement was on the dealer forecourts.

So why were these two not considered better competitors? For starters, the TR5's base price of £1,260 meant that an owner could have nearly three on his driveway for the £3,610 price of one 250 SL. Also, while both engines were fuel injected, the Lucas system in the Triumph quickly gained a reputation for being unpredictable. The Mercedes motor continued to build its reputation for quality, helping to justify its extra cost.

A Swiss advertisement announcing the 250 SL.

On the other side of the power and rarity spectrum was the Bristol 410. The notoriously secretive British company operated in a price class closer to contemporary Aston Martins, with only a fraction of the production. The Bristol was significantly larger and heavier than the 250 SL (and about 40 per cent more expensive) but, with the introduction of the California Coupé, Mercedes was trying to put the Pagoda cars in competition with it.

By this time, Bristol had stopped producing its own engines and was borrowing the 5.2-litre V8 from Chrysler. Having more than double the engine capacity of the 250 SL helped the Bristol 410 to outperform (but only slightly) the Mercedes, which was nearly 500lb (225kg) lighter. The 410's 0–60 time was about 2 seconds quicker than the 250 SL. The Mercedes swing-axle rear suspension was considered downright modern compared with the solid live axle set-up in the Bristol. Still, even as the 250 California Coupé offered 2+2 seating and a removable top that could not be matched by the 410, the Bristol's extra space meant that it was a better grand touring machine for any more than two people.

Someone looking for a low-volume grand touring Brit to compete against the 250 SL might have found a better fit with the last Alvis. The TF21 was the company's swan-song. Its 3.0-litre engine was now upgraded to produce 150bhp and even more torque than the 250 SL. Like the Bristol it came with an ancient solid rear axle, but it was 78lb (35.5kg) lighter than the

250 SL UNFAIR COMPETITION *CONTINUED*

410 and came with the five-speed ZF gearbox as standard. The Alvis certainly looked more traditional than the 250 SL, but its stacked quad headlights and upright grille gave it an appearance somewhere between a Facel Vega and the contemporary Mercedes saloons. The 0–60mph performance was less than 2 seconds slower than the 250 SL and top speed was similar. At £2,670, it undercut both the Bristol and the Mercedes on the UK market.

For those wanting a grand touring machine, the Alvis may have been the choice, while those who wanted better cornering and performance (and who were willing to give up passenger space) may have preferred to upgrade to the 250 SL. Alvis only made 106 TFs before it shut the door on car production at the end of 1967.

The 250 SL was very much a grand touring vehicle.

be mindful to check the rain forecast before setting out on a topless journey.

More Modifications

The 250 SL picked up not only the engine from the 250 SE, but also its braking system. This meant that all 250 SLs were given disc brakes on all four wheels as standard. For the first time in the W113's history there were disc brakes (279mm) in the rear. Up front, since the 250 SE's brakes were larger than those on the 230 SL, the 250 SL upgrade included 0.8in larger discs (273mm). There was also a brake-power regulator installed to ensure even stopping power. The rear brakes each still carried a small drum brake. This was only used as part of the parking brake system and was installed because most companies had not yet figured out how to use discs for adequate hold on hills.

A final drive ratio in the 250 SL went from a 3.75 to a 3.92. In Europe a 3.69 rear-axle reduction was optional. It helped the car accelerate more quickly, but it slightly reduced the top speed, from 124mph (200km/h) to 121mph (195km/h).

The 250 SL had a very modern look when compared with some of the other cars from its era, including the Mercedes 200 model three cars previously.

The variations between the 230 SL and the 250 SL were so manageable that the American publication *Foreign Car Guide* made an interesting observation on its test drive in its December 1967 issue: 'This SL had more than 15,000 miles and nary a quiver to show for months of hard press testing.

The capable independent front suspension with disc brakes remained the same.

The white steering wheel was still a no-cost option.

In fact DB didn't even bother to register a new SL they just simply swapped engines and added the new brake set-up and sent the well-used 230 forth as a 250 SL. Now that's faith in your quality.'

The suspicion of the reviewer cannot be independently confirmed today. The publication date of late 1967 means that there was a window of time during which a press car could have gained 15,000 miles as a brand-new 250 SL. Still, the interchangeability between the two models could easily support *Foreign Car Guide*'s claims. Plus, Mercedes had already been known for some component swapping when creating that early right-hand drive 250 SL for Stirling Moss.

The capacity of the fuel tank was enlarged from 65 litres to 82ltr (from 14.5 to 18gal). This simultaneously increased and decreased the 250 SL's grand touring ability. The added capacity extended the vehicle's range between fill-ups by about 74 to 107 miles. However, the size of the new tank meant that the spare wheel had to go from a vertical position tucked away in the corner of the boot to lying horizontal on the boot floor. The larger tank and new wheel position reduced the luggage capacity by about a third, which meant that the SL may have been able to travel further on one tank of fuel, but weekend vacationers had to pack more carefully for their time away from home.

All the improvements came with a penalty. The 250 SL weighed in at 2,998lb (1,360kg), which was 143lb (65kg) more than the 230 SL.

A Replacement for the 230 SL?

Mercedes was still winding down 230 SL production at the beginning of 1967, with 185 of the 2.3-litre cars being built during that year. In addition, some of the previous year's production of 4,945 230 SLs were still on their way to destinations such as the US and the UK when 250 SL production began. With 230 SLs still making their way to dealers, and the fact that these luxury items inevitably took a little longer to sell, the 230 SL was sticking around for 1967.

Instead of viewing the trickle of remaining 230 SLs as a problem, Mercedes used it as an opportunity. The 250 SL was not marketed as a replacement for a phased-out 230 SL, but instead as a premium upgrade. Mercedes addressed its 230 SL drivers directly in an advertisement introducing the 250 SL: 'Note to 230 SL owners: the 250 SL is not calculated to shunt your car into obsolescence, planned or otherwise. For one thing, it's impossible to tell a 230 SL from a 250 SL without standing about 6 inches from the nameplate and squinting at the lettering. For another, the 230 SL will continue being sold for an indefinite period; the 250 SL's higher price ensures a place for both cars in the showroom.'

Cars that came off at Sindelfingen were shipped around the world, which could mean it would take them many months to reach their final destination.

BATTLING PLANNED OBSOLESCENCE

Planned obsolescence was an idea mastered by the American car industry during the 1950s to the 1970s. In between complete model changeovers, every new model year would see a combination of new styling, more engine power options, and/or more interior features. Rarely would the companies offer any significant changes in the middle of the model year. Thus, car buyers in the USA at this time could rely on deep discounts at the end of the year on annual outgoing models and a reason to justify a purchase on the incoming model year.

Unlike cars from Detroit, it was quite hard to discern the model changes with the 250 SL.

W113 (280 SL) and an interesting foe on the American market, the Cadillac Eldorado.

BATTLING PLANNED OBSOLESCENCE *CONTINUED*

As German car manufacturers were making inroads into the US market during this same period, they had to combat the perceived notion that model years were significant. While Volkswagen made its never-changing style a cornerstone of buying cheap and easy Beetles, this was a slightly more problematic for the premium Mercedes brand. VW was competing in the USA with mainly French and British brands that were also seen as cheap and occasionally restyled, but Mercedes was operating at the other end of the market.

For example, the base 250 SL coupé sold for a few hundred dollars more than the 1967 Cadillac Eldorado, which was $6,277. Whereas the 250 SL was barely distinguishable from the 230 SL, Cadillac's personal luxury vehicle had an all-new exterior – its third change since the W113's debut.

The Chief Executive Officer of Mercedes-Benz of North America, Heinz Hoppe, used engineering as his defence against the unnecessary evolution of American cars. 'We change the exterior only when fundamental internal engineering improvements demand it', he wrote in a letter to prospective buyers in 1965. 'The beauty of a Mercedes speaks for itself, not through gaudy ornamentation or extreme lines. We build cars which are magnificent pieces of machinery, not fashion merchandise.'

The fact is that it would have been almost impossible for Mercedes to keep up with annual changes in the USA, even if it had wanted to do so. During the time of the W113, Mercedes-Benz's smaller output and longer lead time needed for cars to reach every corner of the globe created such situations as the significant overlap in the USA between the 230 and 250 SLs. Mercedes' strategy was to stay true to its form of evolving only as necessary and to market this as a positive selling point. 'We often don't wait for "new model time"', explained Hoppe in the same letter to North American buyers. 'We often don't even announce the improvement. It is immediately built into all new Mercedes.'

And there was no annual sell-off. 'These are not cheap cars', said Hoppe, 'and, quite frankly, your Mercedes dealer won't give you a huge discount on one. He doesn't have to. He isn't burdened with a large inventory of unsold cars.'

The easiest way to tell the difference between the 230 SL and the 250 SL is the boot-lid.

The marketing department's claim about the 230 SL 'being sold for an indefinite period' was a bit of a fib (the actual period of time was destined to last until the stock of 230 SLs ran out), but it made the 230/250 connection quite clear. Another German company of a very different stature, Volkswagen, had been able to break into the US market by assuring customers that its cars did not change every year like the ones from Detroit. This stance against 'planned obsolescence' was finding some favour in the USA, and Mercedes was able to exploit this with the two similar cars.

New Safety Standards

In 1965, Ralph Nader's book *Unsafe At Any Speed* focused on the issues in the US motoring landscape of the time, often citing the Chevrolet Corvair as the chief example. His observations opened the floodgates for consumer complaints in the USA about quality, safety and emissions. The government responded in October 1966 by creating the US Department of Transportation, which in turn created the National Highway Safety Bureau (forerunner of today's National Highway Traffic Safety Administration). Its purpose was to pass rules known as Federal Motor Vehicle Safety Standards, by which any manufacturer selling in the USA was required to abide.

From 1967, the US Government went to work producing a mountain of paperwork relating to new standards in crashworthiness and air quality. As new, tougher rules continued to be passed, car manufacturers both at home and abroad were sent scrambling to find solutions, particularly the importers who were relying on North America as a key sales market.

In Germany, Porsche created the Targa model as a way to build a 911 convertible while still maintaining rollover protection. However, that only alleviated part of their fears. The company's first front-engined model, the 928, was developed out of worries that new USA regulations would eventually outlaw rear-engined cars. If this happened, it would render the entire Porsche line-up illegal in the USA. (The 924 had originally been developed for Audi, and the 914 ran the risk of being classified as rear-engined under new USA regulations.)

Volkswagen was in a similar but more interesting situation. The Beetle was also a named target in Ralph Nader's book.

Mercedes was already at the forefront of automotive safety and testing when the USA began setting new standards.

If safety concerns were not about to kill the little car, its days were numbered anyway. While it had initially been praised for changing very little, by the late 1960s the evergreen personality of the pre-Second World War design was beginning to grow moss. VW nearly replaced the Beetle with another rear-engined concept, but at the last minute it switched to the Golf. Interestingly, the Golf had its engineering roots in an Audi design by Ludwig Kraus – his work on the Mercedes prototype W118 meant that he stayed with Auto Union after the sale to Volkswagen.

Over at Mercedes, safety planning for the USA was less urgent. Although they were still utilizing a rear swing axle just like the Corvair, its low pivot point below the axle tube and transverse compensating spring meant that the Mercedes-Benz cars were quite the opposite of the dangerous Chevy. Actually, Mercedes had been flaunting its safety record years before the publication of Nader's book. The sales literature in 1963 was clear on the subject: 'Fact is, you are safer inside a Mercedes-Benz than most other cars. The rugged pillars and steel roof have withstood rollovers at 40 an hour during exhaustive safety tests.'

When it came to the W113, the majority of the standards put forward by the US Government in 1967 were already met or even exceeded. Even without the pagoda roof, the car was engineered to such a level of strength that no roll bar was needed. It already featured such items as a break-away rear-view mirror, safety steering column, crumple zones and dashboard padding, and other softer surfaces with which a driver might make contact during an accident. Kangol three-point seatbelts became standard on all US-bound cars and optional for other markets. (Retrofitting was also easy in some 230 SLs because mounting points had been in place on the W113 for a few years thanks to UK regulations going back to 1965.)

Despite the presence of all these safety features, some modifications were still necessary to adhere to the new USA standards. In July 1967, all 250 SLs went through a fresh batch of safety improvements, including a stronger door-latch

The low-pivot point and compensating spring in the Mercedes-Benz swing-axle rear end made superior.

The strong design of the W113 meant that it would not require any intrusive bracing to keep passengers safe.

BOTTOM LEFT: **Three-point seatbelts became available for some markets and were standard in the USA.**

assembly to aid in keeping doors operational during accidents, larger outside mirrors, and stronger fuel tank mountings.

The safety steering column was improved so that the shaft and the column would collapse into each other in the event of a front-end collision. This was capped off with a steering wheel that lost some chrome and had some padding added, so that it would be softer during an impact and any distracting reflections would be reduced. Toning down the brightwork on the windscreen wipers and changing the housing on the rear-view mirror from chrome to black further reduced glare.

Padding was also added to the windscreen frame. The locking latches that stuck out from the headliner directly in front of the two front-seat occupants could now be removed and stored in an included glovebox pouch. The turn signal/wiper/flasher stalk became longer. Control knobs and switches (including the heater controls and window cranks) were built to be more elastic. A brake-fluid warning light was added. A plaque was added to the heater controls to explain

Under new **US** regulations, major components had to be labelled, so a diagram showing the heater operation was added.

The interior was revised to reduce glare.

their operation. The pop-out safety glass on the windscreen was also improved, with better high-impact glazing.

Inside the door, the combination armrest/map pocket was changed specifically for the US market. The unit was now separated to accommodate a soft pouch to replace the hard pocket, and this allowed for a large and softer armrest to be bolted to the door. For European markets, the item continued without a change.

Other USA-specific changes included the addition of side reflectors, yellow on the front fenders and red on the rear. The '0' used to symbol neutral on automatic transmission selectors was replaced with the more standardized 'N' (and this would spread to worldwide production by the next year).

The most significant changes on the W113 relating to the new US regulations were in the engine compartment. The move from 2.3 to 2.5 litres was intended to keep Mercedes-Benz's top passenger sports car with its six-cylinder and give some more torque to the popular automatic transmission option. Meanwhile, in the US market, which had been accustomed to huge horsepower from enormous engines, the new regulations zapped power to

the point that the same large motors were needed just to keep the heavy metal moving. As the USA continued down the path of improving air quality through detuning engines, the regulations would soon erase any power improvements gained in the 250 SL.

A Short Life

The new US regulations were not the only problem for the 250 SL. Many W113 owners who had manual transmissions, or who were habitually overriding their automatics, would argue that the 230 SL was a better car than the 250 SL. Since the 230 SL had to be performance-tuned for its 150bhp, the drive was more rewarding. Although the flatter torque curve of the 250 SL made it the darling of the automatics, enthusiasts sometimes found the 230 SL's aggressive engine more appealing.

The argument over which car was better would be a 1967-only discussion. While it took nearly 4 years for the W113 to get its first power upgrade, the 250 SL would be obsolete within a year.

1968 brought a new sedan generation and the end of the 250 SL.

250 SL OPTIONS AT LAUNCH

Item	Cost (DM)
Automatic radio antenna	210
(without radio installed)	240
(manual without radio installed)	40
Right-side mirror	15
Coupé roof	1,180
without soft top	400
without soft top but with rear bench (California Coupé)	510
'D' badge	3
Suppression for radio installation	60
Sport springs	12
Fire extinguisher	60
Luggage rack	290
Four-speed automatic gearbox	1,400
Five-speed ZF manual gearbox	
(requires 4.08 rear axle ratio)	1,200
Cabin light	60
3.69 rear axle	no charge
Fitted luggage	
1 large suitcase, 2 medium suitcases (package)	295
large suitcase	105
medium suitcase	85
small suitcase	89
hat suitcase	55

Item	Cost (DM)
toiletry bag	80
leather strap	20
Coco floor mats	40
Two-tone paint (monochrome)	no charge
Two-tone paint (metallic body)	400
Two-tone paint (metallic roof)	170
Ivory steering wheel	no charge
Leather upholstery	800
Rear transverse seat (MB-Tex)	200
Rear transverse seat (leather)	250
Radio – Becker Grand Prix	650
Radio – Becker Mexico	630
Radio – Becker Europa	490
Whitewall tyres	175
All-season tyres	240
Power steering	550
Seatbelts (driver and passenger)	110
Ski rack	135
First aid kit	30
Upgraded heat exchanger	20
Tinted windows	
front and side (roadster)	70
front and side (coupé)	60
front, side, and rear (coupé)	105
Decorative coupé roof bars necessary for mounting roof racks	40
Towbar	dealer install

250 SL

Steel unibody with aluminium doors, boot and bonnet

Engine
Name	M 129 III (type 129.982)
Block material	cast iron
Head material	aluminium
Cylinders	inline 6

Engine continued

Cooling	water	
Bore and stroke	82 x 78.8mm	
Capacity	2496cc	
Valves	12v sohc	
Compression ratio	9.5:1	
Fuel system	manifold-injection, mechanically controlled, Bosch 6-plunger fuel injection	
Max. power	150bhp @ 5,500rpm (DIN)	170bhp @5,600 (SAE)
Max. torque	160lb/ft @ 4,200rpm (DIN)	174lb/ft @4,500rpm (SAE)
Fuel capacity	82ltr (18gal)	

Transmission

Gearbox Clutch	four-speed manual	four-speed automatic	five-speed manual
Ratios	dry single-plate	fluid coupling	dry single-plate
1st	4.05	3.98	3.92
2nd	2.23	2.52	2.22
3rd	1.4	1.58	1.42
4th	1	1	1
5th	NA	NA	0.85
Reverse	3.58	4.15	3.49
Final drive	3.92 (3.69 optional)	3.92 (3.69 optional)	4.08

Performance

Top speed	121mph/195km/h (3.92), 124mph/200km/h (RA 3.69)	118mph/190km/h (3.92), 121mph/195km/h (RA 3.69)	124mph/200km/h
0–62mph (100km/h)	10 sec	10.6 sec	9.7 sec

Suspension and Steering

Front	double wishbone, coil springs, torsion bar stabilizer
Rear	single-joint swing axle with compensating spring, coil springs
Steering	recirculating-ball (power optional)
Tyres	185 HR 14
Wheels	steel
Rim width	6 J x 14 HB

Brakes

Type	hydraulic dual-circuit brake system with vacuum booster; disc brakes all four wheels
Size	10.7-in front, 11-in rear

Dimensions

Track			
front	58.42in, 1,484mm	Overall width	69.3in, 1,760mm
rear	58.46in, 1,485mm	Overall height	52in, 1,320mm
Wheelbase	94.5in, 2,400mm	Unladen weight	2,998lb, 1,360kg
Overall length	168.7in, 4,285mm		

CHAPTER TEN

280 SL

In November 1967, just one year after the 250 SL had begun its pilot run, the 280 SL entered the assembly line at Sindelfingen. The tipping point in the creation of this car was the need for larger engine capacities to keep up with the emissions regulations in Mercedes-Benz's most important export market, the USA. The by-product of this quest for more power was the best-selling version of the W113.

Moving From 2.5 to 2.8

In hindsight, 250 SL was just a stepping-stone on the route to the development of the 280 SL. Mercedes was already complying with the new safety standards in the USA, but it was now being affected by emissions requirements, too. A car like the W113 already had to prove itself worthy on

A familiar face to any W113 owner.

All engines were tested before leaving the factory.

that market while being called underpowered, and it would not help the car if Mercedes had to offer less power than in previous years.

Stricter emissions regulations were enforced in the USA for 1968. The initial standards had a multi-tier system designed to curb the emissions of larger engines. The 250 SL's motor was only 0.2ltr over the line into the highest displacement class. This meant that if Mercedes installed any larger engines in the SL, they would be held to the same to 275ppm (part per million) in unburned hydrocarbon emissions.

Mercedes did not need to continue to re-invent its inline six engine every few years. It was already well evolved when it went from four to seven main bearings in the 250 SL. As a result, when the company began to look for extra grunt for the 280 SL, enlarging the M 129 III engine block was the basis for the upgrade to the M 130. The motor in the 250 SL was bored out 4.5mm. This enlargement made the spacing between cylinder banks more uniform and improved the engine-cooling management. Efficiency was also on the engineers' minds as the cylinder head and combustion chamber were revised to provide better overall emissions.

280 SL at the Mercedes-Benz test track in Untertürkheim.

The result was that the W113 now offered 170bhp DIN (180bhp SAE in the USA). Unlike the previous two Pagoda SLs, whose power peaked at 5,500rpm (5,600 in the USA), the 280 SL would hit its extra horsepower at 5,750rpm. As might be expected, peak torque also raised, from 4,200 to 4,500rpm.

One of the complaints from 250 SL owners was that, while the engine may have had more torque than the 230 SL, it felt like the 230 was allowed to work harder for its power and was, therefore, livelier than the 250. To help rectify this, Mercedes gave the 2.8-litre engine a new camshaft that allowed a more sporting rev range than the 250 SL. This profile provided the most significant difference a customer could feel between the 280 SL and the 2.8-litre/170bhp motor that went into the upper-level saloons.

2.8-litre in the USA

As with the previous engines in the W113, the US-market version of the 280 SL had more horsepower listed than the

level that was being offered in other parts of the world. The variation in power ratings between the USA and the rest of the world went deeper than a mere difference between DIN and SAE; the difference between net and gross gave the USA an inflated power ratings system. But there was an extra discrepancy with the 280 SL.

While European models jumped from 150 to 170bhp (a 13.25 per cent difference) with the 250 SL to 280 SL change-over, the US-bound cars went from 170 to 180bhp (a 5.75 per cent difference). New emissions regulations meant that engines bound for the USA had a separate block designation. They also included a milder camshaft for less valve overlap combined with recalibration to the fuel-injection system for a leaner burn. This not only cut into the extra power from the 2.8-litre engine, but it also made the motor run hotter. As a result, US-spec cars received a larger cooling system from the outset; this system would be used on all 280 SLs by 1969.

The power difference did not go unnoticed in America. Magazines reviewing the 280 SL referred to a hotter 195bhp engine that was available in other parts of the world but not in their market. This mysterious motor was simply the

ABOVE: **A very American 280 SL, with sealed headlamps and bumper guards.**

Regardless of the market, the view from behind the wheel of the 280 SL was quite similar to that of its predecessors in the W113 lifespan.

280 SL – UNFAIR COMPETITION

At the beginning of the Pagoda SL's lifecycle, it was in a class by itself, and even in its twilight years, in 1971, in a market that was notably changed, its individuality remained a significant factor. The USA was still an important export market, but its needs had become quite different. The W113 had been born at the beginning of the era of the muscle car but by the time of its swansong, it was being choked by emissions regulations.

Jaguar's E-Type was still prowling around the 280 SL, but it had just entered its weighty Series III form. The E-Type was still a better bargain than the 280 SL, but now the 5.3-litre V12 was thirstier and all the changes made the roadster heavier than the 280 SL.

In addition to the E-Type, there was now a better contender from England – the Triumph Stag was a newcomer to the grand touring market. Its handsomely conservative design seemed to be so aligned with the 280 SL customer that Triumph specifically targeted the Mercedes in its advertising. While both were available with a soft hood and a removable hard top, the reality was that these were very different cars. The Stag may have had a 3.0-litre V8, but its 145bhp undercut the 280 SL. The $5,300 base price was about 30 per cent less than the 280 SL Roadster. Throw in overheating issues and Triumph's less than prestigious brand image, and the Stag proved to be more of a pretender than a contender.

Not long after the introduction of the W113, Porsche decided to join the modern world, with the 911. By the time the 280 SL was finishing its run, the evergreen Porsche was just beginning to hit its stride. The 911 was offered in enough engine variations that it was able to bracket in the 280 SL on both price and power. Even the new Targa model seemed to blend some of the ideas of the hard/soft top combination available on the Coupé/Roadster SL. As a result, the 911 may have been the 280 SL's closest competitor. Although this may seem odd, considering the Mercedes was firmly aimed at the luxury market and the Porsche was more track-focused, both cars offered a feeling of precision that could only come from Teutonic engineers.

Some argued that the 280 SL faced domestic competition on the American market from the Chevrolet Corvette. In 1971, Chevrolet was still able to use engine size to combat some emissions regulations. The Corvette could be as pricey as the 280 SL – reaching the $7,469 base price of the Mercedes – but only with just about every option box ticked on the order sheet. Consumers who were interested in spending Mercedes-type money could have a 7.3-litre 425bhp V8 Corvette. However, it was unlikely that the kind of driver who admired the near-silent tick-over of the 280 SL would be drawn to the raucous.

The W113 almost carries two different styling personalities – with and without its famous hard top.

unregulated 2.8-litre engine with its power listed in Ameri-canized SAE.

Transmission options were carried over from the 250 SL, including no change in ratios for the standard four-speed manual or the available four-speed automatic and five-speed manual unit. Final drive ratio also held to 3.92:1, or 3.69:1 for the four-speed cars and 4.08:1 for the five-speed. The major exception to this was in America, where the cars once again received special consideration, with a standard 4.08 rear end standard for all transmissions (eventually this would change to 3.92).

Servicing Issues

US rules and regulations might have been the catalyst for the development of the 2.8-litre 280 SL, but changes to the engine were not the only concession made by Mercedes-Benz for its largest export market. Servicing was a significant source of complaint for Pagoda owners in the USA. The 2,000-mile

(3,200-km) intervals for the 230 and 250 SLs were as much as three times more frequent than those that American consumers were used to, even in the luxury market.

The problem was compounded by the lack of availability of Mercedes service outlets. In 1965 Mercedes had 231 dealers in the continental USA, compared with, for example, the American luxury brand Lincoln, which had about twice as many during the same period. US consumers who had switched from a domestic product to a W113 were a bit shocked to have to have their new car serviced that much more often, especially since the dealer was likely to be further away.

To help resolve this issue, Mercedes took many of the original 21 steering and suspension components that required greasing and swapped them for sealed units. This included replacing many brushings for rubber joints. The changes allowed the manufacturer to extend the service intervals to 6,000 miles (or about 10,000km), but some drivers complained of a loss in the spirited sports car grip, which had been replaced by grand touring comfort.

The Bosch Lichteinheit can give the headlights a jewel-like quality in the right light.

Mercedes-Benz 280 SL:
Sportlicher als manche Sportwagen.
Und komfortabler als viele Limousinen.

Mercedes-Benz   Ihr guter Stern auf allen Straßen

German advertisement reminding the potential buyer
that the 280 SL is sportier than some sports cars and
more comfortable than many sedans.

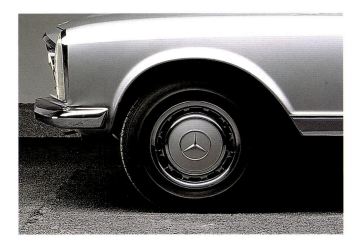

The standard wheel changed to the full cover shared
with the W114.

An opposite downside was felt when Mercedes switched from the specialty Firestone and Continental tyres to conventional radials. The W113 initially came with the hybrid tyres to combine the comfort of cross-ply rubber with the track-friendly grip of radials. Advances in radial-tyre technology made them a bit more comfortable by the time the 280 SL came along, so those who mostly drove their car on rough roads (or read the enthusiast car magazines) really felt this change.

(Incidentally, Mercedes seemed to have the right strategy about extending the service intervals instead of creating new outlets across America. Since the first year of MBNA in 1966, the dealer network expanded by only about 100 more franchises over the next five decades. During that time, sales would increase 20-fold, to 261,808 annually. Over a similar period, Lincoln was forced to reduce its dealer network down to similar levels to Mercedes, having seen its annual figures slump to about a third of the German rival over the years.)

More Changes and Options

Where the exterior difference between the 230 SL and 250 SL could be seen only on the boot-lid, there was an extra clue on the 280 SL. The wheels were changed to the same ones that were available on the W114 saloons. On the 230 and 250 SLs, running inwards from the tyre was a chrome trim ring, a colour ring from the exposed steel wheel, and the chrome ring and a solid colour centre of the hubcap. The wheels on the 280 SL had a chrome ring (vented) with a solid colour centre. It was hardly a drastic change, but it will help the 280 SL-spotter at car auctions.

Towards the end of the 280 SL's life, it got its first set of optional wheels. From August 1970, owners could choose Barockfelgen ('Baroque wheels'), lightweight alloy units manufactured by Fuchs. While these wheels were not often seen on the Pagoda SLs, they would become iconic on Mercedes cars in the 1970s and 80s.

Few features were added to the options list during the lifecycle of the 230 SL or the short-lived 250 SL, but the 280 SL would gain a few interesting items. It started out with many of the same options as its predecessors, but by the summer of 1968 (still in the 280 SL's first full year), the equipment list began to get a little longer. In June, a heat/defrost option began to appear for the coupé roof (although

Optional safety headrests would become a recognizable feature of Mercedes-Benz cars for decades to come.

it would not be until April 1969 that its official price of DM 190 first appeared). Detachable headrests were a safety add-on that appeared as early as October 1968, in a choice of leather, MB-Tex, vinyl or fabric; eventually the choice was narrowed down to just leather or MB-Tex. Another safety option of a rear fog light would become available from spring of 1969.

One of the more technologically advanced options offered that did not come directly from the Mercedes engineers was a Becker or TeKaDe car telephone. By far the most expensive add-on ever offered for the W113, it commanded DM 7,400 when it first appeared on the option list in April 1969. On a car that started at DM 23,255, being able to talk on the go would add almost another third on to the price. This option would prove to be a relative bargain, however, compared with the 280 SL's final price list a few years later. By then, the cost of the phone had risen to DM 9,935, representing a premium of more than 37 per cent over the car's DM 26,640 base price.

While US demands and regulations dictated many changes to the W113, at least one modification went in the opposite direction. In 1969 the tail lights, which were nearly solid red (except for the lower mid-section for the reversing light), were given better functionality by colouring the side turning light amber. This was first started in Europe and would migrate to North America by the end of the year.

Headlight options occasionally provide clues to a 280 SL's age. A round halogen fog-light set, mounted next to the standard light unit, first appeared on the option list in the summer of 1968 and had disappeared by the spring of 1970. The fog lights' placement in front of the 280 SL's grille is hard to miss. Although they never looked like they were part of an original design plan, they were far from out of place. These lights appeared across the Mercedes passenger car line-up. The curved glass of the Bosch Lichteinheits were changed slightly in March 1970. At this time, the optional fog lights that were mounted in front of the grille were moved to reside behind this updated unit.

The US market had its own headlight unit, and the ever-changing conditions in the country would lead to multiple subtle modifications during the life of 280 SL. The part number for US-bound 230 SL headlights was LE 1657 AC. This housed the round sealed halogen light at the top and then filled the rest of the area designed for the Lichteinheits with a form-fitting piece of glass that also included space for a fog light and an amber turn indicator. In 1968, these 'AC' lenses were replaced with ones that had the 'AN' suffix. The outline of the housing did not change much on the new piece; the difference was that the lower section was missing its fog light, which had been replaced with a full amber section. Then, in 1969, the outside side reflectors were changed for lighted units. As part of this modification, Mercedes swapped

ABOVE: **This 280 SL has quite a few option boxes checked, as it includes two-tone paint, a bench seat (California Coupé), and a power radio antenna.**

New tail lights gain colour for better function.

The difference in US-spec headlights during the 280 SL.

'AN' lights for 'AJ' ones, which provided wiring support to the newly illuminated side markers and also made the amber section on the headlights more predominant.

In case the unique headlights were not enough to distinguish US-spec cars, some of the 280 SLs exported across the Atlantic were also fitted with bumper guards. Although standards for front and rear protection would not be enforced until 1973, Mercedes made this feature available ahead of any requirement. The vertical metal pieces with black rubber fronts have rarely been considered attractive, but they were less intrusive than the items that would be used on the next SL.

The final difference for the USA would be in weight. While US-bound 250 SLs were rumoured to be packing a few extra pounds, it was much more apparent in the 280 SL. The cars for the rest of the world held steady at 2,998lb (1,362kg) but the extra regulations for the USA added about 120lb (55kg). This kind of gain could occasionally be felt behind the wheel, but the 280 SL was still somewhat svelte compared with developments elsewhere in the Mercedes line.

V8s and Rotary Power for the W113

It was not just the Americans who were looking for more power from Mercedes; pressure was starting to build up at home, too. After identifying a lack of large-displacement vehicles at Opel and Mercedes in 1967, German magazine *Auto Motor und Sport*, was puzzled: 'Daimler-Benz does have a state-of-the-art eight-cylinder design which leads a respectable life in the 600 behind closed doors as it were, but it is hard to understand why a smaller-displacement version of this engine has not long since been installed in the intermediate range saloon. This should not be asking too much of Germany's most renowned automobile manufacturers at a time when Ford comes home victorious from Le Mans using simple mass-produced eight-cylinder engines.'

The argument did not fall on deaf ears at Mercedes-Benz. Research engineer Erich Waxenberger took the 6.3-litre V8 (M 100) motor out of the 600 Grand Mercedes and installed it in a W109 coupé body. Waxenberger was eager to get behind the wheel of this 250bhp (DIN) stealth sports car, which had 47 per cent more power than the 300 SE's 3.0-litre M 189 engine. He was the first one to test the V8 coupé, and drove the car around the Mercedes headquarters testing grounds long into the evening.

The next morning, Waxenberger's boss Rudolf Uhlenhaut called him into his office. Uhlenhaut, who was already well known for his performance mind, was intrigued about a car with a striking engine note that had been driven past his office window the night before. This car would evolve into the 300 SEL 6.3, the world's most powerful saloon car at the time – but the story did not end there.

Waxenberger was key in testing the W113 for rallying, and he prepared the SLs for their 1963 and 1964 races.

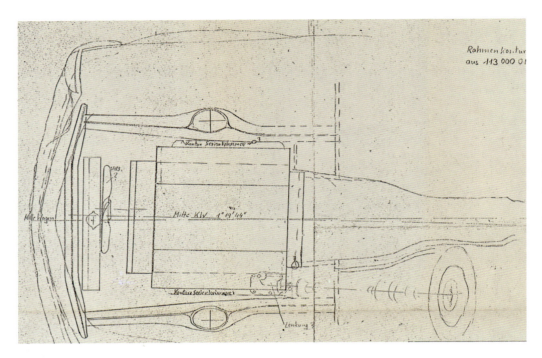

LEFT AND BOTTOM: **Drawing from above and the side of the 6.3-litre V8 engine M100 from the 600 saloon installed in the W113.**

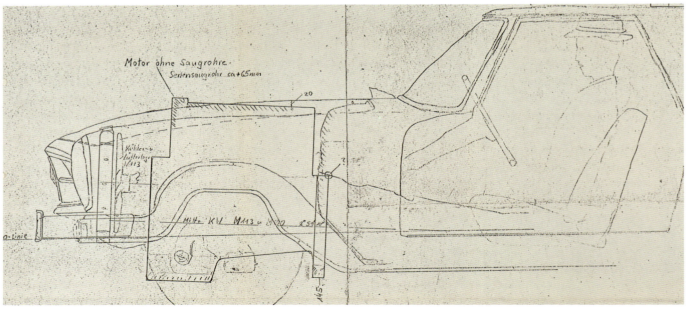

He was known at Mercedes for enjoying a challenge and being a problem solver. After installing Mercedes-Benz's only V8 into the W109 line, he focused his attention on the Pagoda cars.

The W113 would present a particular challenge for the large V8. The standard inline six-cylinder motor was already a snug fit for the engine compartment and the frame of the donor W113 had to be welded to accommodate the new length and width of the larger eight-cylinder engine. Many key components also had to be relocated. From the outside, however, it was hard to distinguish this powerful prototype Pagoda from the production breed. The only real giveaway was the significantly wider bulge on the bonnet, which deserved its 'powerdome' nickname.

Waxenberger had the V8 Pagoda finished by the summer of 1967, and between 3 and 5 July he tested this prototype at the Nürburgring north loop. The car was equipped with an automatic transmission, steel springs, stiff shocks, and Dunlop racing tyres (with the rear wheel camber adjusted between minus 4 degrees 30 minutes and minus 5 degrees).

In the hands of the capable Waxenberger, the V8 Pagoda achieved lap times of between 10 minutes 40 seconds and 11 minutes 6 seconds.

While the lap times were easily the best for any Pagoda SL, the car was not without its faults. The V8 motor added a noticeable amount of weight to the Pagoda. The front racing tyres wore out after nine laps, while the rear rubber would hold out for sixteen laps. During heavy braking, the front dive that was known to all Pagodas was further exaggerated on the nose-heavy V8 car. In addition, the extra power and inertia would require further development of the rear swing axle, which Mercedes was already phasing out. In the end, it was decided that the large motor was not right for a car that had such a good reputation for being well balanced. The prototype was destroyed by the factory.

Although the V8 was not right for the W113, this was not the last time that Mercedes would test more powerful motors for its SL. Only a year after the prototype V8 Pagoda had its days at the Nürburgring, the head of engine development, Wolf-Dieter Bensinger, would use the 280 SL as a

280 SL test car installed with the 6.3-litre from the 600 saloon.

Three-rotor Wankel engine used in the Pagoda and the first version of the C111.

testbed for the Wankel engine. This official prototype would be known as W33-29.

This three-rotor, 3.4-litre unit was more compact than the 6.3-litre V8, so it caused fewer installation problems. Although quite a bit smaller than the eight-cylinder engine, the rotary was rated at 203bhp and achieved a top speed of 127mph (203km/h), 6mph (almost 10km/h) more than a production 280 SL. Between 18 June and 23 October 1968, test drivers would rack up 43,875 miles (69,000km) on local roads and race circuits in the Wankel Pagoda.

Prototype W33-29 was the forerunner for the more famous C111 research vehicle, which appeared in 1969. Mercedes would soon abandon the Wankel-engine projects, and no Pagoda SL ever left the production line with anything other than the inline six-cylinder engines. This helped the cars retain a well-balanced driving feel, but the world around the W113 was changing.

Changing the Pagoda's Perception

The W113 spent much of the 1960s powered by some of the best engines Mercedes had to offer. They were not always of the largest capacity, but the Pagoda cars did occupy the upper echelon of the level of speed that Mercedes had available for consumer vehicles. The introduction of the 300 SEL 6.3 was the signal that Mercedes was beginning to aim for a higher engine capacity for future consumer cars.

Mercedes-Benz went head first into the V8 market in the 1970s. As the number of available V8s doubled (with the 4.5-litre for the regulation-restricted US market and the 3.5-litre for the rest of the world), the inline six in the 280 SL was now running in the middle of the Mercedes pack. The media did not expect the only sports car from Mercedes to remain this low on power for very long. In

C111 – THE MISTAKEN W113 SUCCESSOR

The C111-I research vehicle was debuting at about the same time as the 300 SEL 3.5 and the 280 SE 3.5 coupé and convertible. With Mercedes marketing premium sedans alongside the gullwing prototype, it is easy to understand how the public could see the C111 as the next evolution of the SL.

There was an exciting surprise on the Mercedes-Benz stand at the Frankfurt Motor Show in September 1969. The company that was currently producing very crisp, squared-off designs was featuring a sleek, wedge-shaped sports car painted in a bright orange hue they called *weissherbst*. The C111 stole the show.

Although the W113 had not yet even celebrated its seventh birthday, it was not hard for the public to see a future SL in this concept car. The C111 had the speedy good looks that could have easily been the evolution of the original 300 SL, and the new car's gullwing doors only solidified this view. Mercedes maintained this car was only a testbed for technology, but that did not stop speculation, especially in *The Mercedes-Benz Star* club newsletter, autumn 1969 edition: 'Not only do the new car and the old one have doors hinged at the top, but when the first 300 SLs were built they were also strictly experimental.'

Four-rotor Wankel engine inside the C111-II.

C111 – THE MISTAKEN W113 SUCCESSOR *CONTINUED*

Mercedes was sincere about the C111 being a testbed and not a SL design study. The orange machine was born out of Mercedes-Benz's desire to experiment with glas- fibre bodywork. Underneath the plastic skin was a three-rotor Wankel motor that developed 280bhp. It could propel the lightweight car from 0–62mph in 5 seconds and top out at 162mph (160km/h).

No matter how much Mercedes denied that the C111 was anything other than a 'test lab on wheels', the enthusiast community could not dismiss the concept so quickly. The car appeared in plenty of Mercedes-Benz press material, including photos that featured nearly a full passenger-car line-up minus the W113. It was easy to believe that this new gullwing had in fact already replaced the Pagoda.

Although it had an ultra-modern appearance for the early 1970s, the doors of the C111 instantly linked the C111 to Mercedes heritage (version II seen here).

The excitement over the C111 had not died down when Mercedes appeared at the next major car show with an improved version. The C111-II, which debuted at the Geneva Motor Show in March 1970, retained the wedge shape and gullwing doors, but had better aerodynamics. What really set the C111-II apart was a new four-rotor Wankel engine that produced 350bhp. The 0–62mph time had was improved to 4.8 seconds and the top speed was now 186mph (298km/h).

At this point it was hard not to view this as a possible SL car. Where Mercedes originally found it tough to replace the 300 SL with a competitive sports car, the C111-II had better performance figures than contemporary cars such as the Ferrari Daytona and the Lamborghini Miura. In Stuttgart, Mercedes was receiving orders for this new car, complete with promises for down payments and blank cheques.

While the pre-order strategy had worked to get the 300 SL on the road, it would not work for the C111 project. The rotary engine was powerful, but it was proving to be unreliable and inefficient. According to Dr Hans Liebold, the engineer responsible for the C111 project, 'The Wankel engine was not yet mature enough to be handed over to customers in line with company standards.'

It was this same view that killed the rotary motor versions of the W113 and R107 SLs. The C111 project would live on with diesel motors. These cars would capture endurance speed records throughout the 1970s, but no version was ever badged SL or offered to the public.

Mercedes-Benz C111 prototype (version II seen here) testing at the Stuttgart headquarters in 1970.

Das neue Mercedes-Benz Programm der großen Sechszylinder.

Was an den großen Mercedes-Benz Sechs-zylinder-Modellen besticht, ist ihre aus-gefeilte Automobiltechnik.

Ausgefeilte Technik aber kann man nicht sehen, man kann sie nur erleben. Beim Fahren.

Dazu laden wir Sie ein.

Nach einer Probefahrt wissen Sie, was diese repräsentativen Wagen wirk-lich repräsentieren: perfekte Automobil-technik. Eine optimale Kombination von Schnelligkeit, Sicherheit, Komfort und Zuverlässigkeit.

Ohne Probefahrt kann man nicht mitreden. Rufen Sie uns bitte an.

Mercedes-Benz
Ihr guter Stern auf allen Straßen

Die neue Mercedes-Benz Generation		
Typ	Motor	PS (DIN)
250 S	6-Zylinder	130
280 S	6-Zylinder	140
280 SE*	6-Zylinder	160
300 SEL	6-Zylinder	170
280 SL	6-Zylinder	170

*auch als Cabriolet und Coupé. Außer-dem als 280 SE mit langem Radstand.

Walter Schmidt · Vertreter der Daimler-Benz AG · 24 Lübeck · Fackenburger Allee 66 · Telefon 4 24 41/44

German advertisement touting the six-cylinder programme during the period when the 280 SL and the 300 SEL shared the 2.8-litre motor and same power figure. Of course, the 6.3 V8 stuffed into the sedan would keep it as the flagship.

autumn 1968 *Motor Trend* magazine got wind of the new eight-cylinder motors making their way into some of the Mercedes cars. It could not wait to imagine the possibili-ties, although its prediction was somewhat inaccurate: 'It's interesting to speculate on how the 280 SL will perform with the new, big V8 and altered suspension it will get some time in the future.'

Instead, the Pagoda cars were once again beginning to live up to their Sport Leicht ('sport lightweight') namesake, if only because they were carrying a more moderate mass than other cars from Mercedes. That is somewhat ironic consid-ering their own weight problems earlier, but they were not tipping the scales quite as severely as some other cars in the line-up. For example, in 1968, when the 280 SL was entering its first full model year, it weighed in at 2,998lb (1,363kg), plus an extra 120lb (55kg) for the USA. This was about 175

to 240lb (80–110kg) less than the 2.5- and 2.8-litre saloons that made up the top end of the Mercedes line-up at the time. The 300 SEL that shared the 280 SL's engine was a whopping 570lb (260kg) heavier; it only found 2,519 takers worldwide over a short run.

Fast-forward to 1971 and the last full year of the W113. The 280 SL is holding steady with its weight, but its surround-ings have changed. The 250 model line is phased out. The 280 saloons still use the 2.8-litre inline six as a base, but the 3.5- and 4.5-litre V8s now join them. The extra weight tagged on to the upgrade makes the eight-cylinder 280 saloons 428–759lb (195–345kg) heavier than the 280 SL, depending on the market and specification. The top-end 300 SEL is no longer available with a 2.8-litre engine; this is replaced by the 3.5- and 4.5-litre units, making the cars 594 and 869lb (270 and 395kg) heavier than the 280 SL respectively. Basically,

1969 Mercedes-Benz 280 SE 3.5 Cabriolet.

over the life of the 280 SL, the difference in weight between it and the upper end of Mercedes saloons went from a moderately sized person to an entire carload!

These new V8s both came with the added bonus of about 17 per cent more horsepower, and a 19 per cent gain in torque for the 3.5-litre and 49 per cent gain in the 4.5-litre. This meant these new saloons were quick, and Mercedes engineers worked their magic on the suspension to keep them nimble, but they still dispelled any myths that Mercedes did not build tanks.

None of these higher-power V8s would make it into the production W113. Mercedes had envisioned the Pagoda models as comfortable sports cars, not Ferrari rivals, so they would always keep the sprightlier six-cylinder engines.

Asking For More

The press feedback on the W113 followed the car's progress a bit like that of an athlete. The 230 SL was the youngster who matured from having something to prove to being a superstar. The 250 SL was the year the athlete showed something a little extra and the 280 SL represented the twilight years. The 280 was juiced up in order to stay competitive with the younger pack coming up, but it would not last. By 1970, the media's view of the W113 was that it was still a hero worthy of being on the playing field, but its days of superstar status were over.

The British magazine *Autocar* noted in its September review that the automatic transmission 'held on to a lower ratio longer than we would have liked, and with no torque converter to cushion the drive line the quality of the kick-down changes was often rather jerky'. It seemed that the

While the W113 is an icon of timeless style, the gentleman behind the wheel is a bit dated for this publicity shot.

magazine was no longer impressed with the ability to shift the automatic transmission. 'In 1964 we said this transmission was among the best in our experience and so it was. Since then everyone else has improved theirs and even Mercedes have a better one, which surprisingly they do not fit in this car. By 1970 standards it is therefore only good in parts.'

The article went on to comment on an engine that was a bit overmatched, and then it turned its attention to the suspension: 'The 280 SL is very stable at speed in a straight line, but we found it needed small corrections when taking a sweeping bend at speed and lacked the positive feel of something like the Jaguar XJ6 or Aston Martin DBS.' Both the Jaguar and the Aston Martin debuted years after the W113.

Autocar's phrasing may have been somewhat dated, but the article did conclude by recognizing the 280 SL's merits: 'At just over £5,000 it is far from cheap, and in a few ways it is beginning to show the age of the original concept. Yet from behind the wheel one feels that in its engineering alone it is worth the money and at the top end of the two-seater market it has barely a single rival in the world.'

America's *Road and Track* was also a fan of the 280 SL, but knew its time was limited. The reviewer first got his hands on the 280 SL for the August 1968 edition and declared, 'In the matter of handling, brakes and ride the SL is still one of the outstanding cars of the day.' However, as the article continued, it was clear that this was not the same W113 they

The optional rear transverse seat carried only half as many occupants as the rear bench but its less intrusive nature allowed owners to keep the well for the cloth hood.

had once known: 'The single-pivot swing axles at the rear don't give quite the adhesion that a more up-to-date system would, so that's it's easy to tweak out the rear end. The big sticky Firestone Phoenix radial tires give fairly high cornering limits, but it's obvious that the added torque of the 280 engine brings this venerable suspension close to the end of its usefulness.'

A Sales Darling

The automotive media may have not been too kind to the 280 SL, but that did not seem to hinder sales. The 280 SL's three full years of production, 1968, 1969 and 1970, were the three most significant sales years for the W113, with total production numbers of 6,930, 8,047 and 7,935 respectively. The batch of 143 cars produced in the first couple of months of 1967, and the final cars that rolled off the assembly line up to March 1971 (830 cars), all add up to a grand total of 23,855 280 SLs produced. Although the 230 SL had a longer run than the 280 SL, the 280's popularity meant that it

accounted for nearly half (49 per cent) of the 48,912 W113s ever produced.

Key to this success story was the USA. Of all the W113s sold, 49 per cent were distributed through MBNA; more specifically, 70 per cent of all 280 SLs went to North America. In turn, the W113 gave the Mercedes-Benz a strong positioning in the USA as sales climbed during the full production years of the Pagoda, from 11,296 to 29,108 cars annually. Interestingly, 18.5 per cent of this growth occurred during the period of the 280 SL alone.

The Pagoda's era was one of the most interesting and turbulent times since the birth of the automobile. Some of the most graceful designs were coming out of Europe and in America there was a horsepower explosion. But safety and emissions regulations would bring the party to an end on an international scale.

This was the beginning of a new era, and, while the Pagoda could still live with the regulations, changes needed to be made to keep the SL at the forefront of the Mercedes line-up. There were a few studies aimed at modifying the W113 to make it less expensive to build and to give it more

Béla Barényi posing with the first sports car to utilize his safety ideas – the W113.

power, but that kind of change would have ruined its soul. Joe Oldham, writing in the magazine *Hi-Performance Imported Cars*, understood the appeal of this car: 'If the 280 SL were a woman, she would be a Lufthansa airline stewardess – beautiful in a blond-haired, blue-eyed Teutonic sort of way and utterly efficient if somewhat cold at everything including sex. But she would be the kind of woman you could fall in love with – very easily. And that's the kind of car the 280 SL is. It's very easy to fall in love with it even though you know its shortcomings.'

280 SL OPTIONS AT LAUNCH

Item	Cost (DM)		
Automatic radio antenna	195	without soft top but with rear	
(without radio installed)	225	bench (leather)	605
(manual without radio installed)	38	'D' badge	3
Limited slip rear differential	150	Suppression for radio installation	55
Right side mirror		Sport springs	11
or	14	Fire extinguisher	55
Coupé roof	1,120	Luggage rack	265
without soft top	389	Four-speed automatic gearbox	1,300
without soft top but with rear		Five-speed ZF manual gearbox	
bench (MB-Tex)	485	(requires 4.08 rear axle ratio)	1,120
		Cabin light	55

Item	Cost (DM)		
3.69 rear axle	no charge	Rear transverse seat (MB-Tex)	190
Fitted luggage		Rear transverse seat (leather)	235
1 large suitcase, 2 medium suitcases		Radio – Becker Grand Prix	650
(package)	264	Radio – Becker Mexico	630
1 large suitcase, 1 medium suitcase,		Radio – Becker Europa	490
1 hat suitcase (package)	231	Whitewall radial tyres	165
1 large suitcase, 2 medium suitcases,		All-season tyres	35
1 toiletry suitcase (package)	371	Power steering	510
large suitcase	97	Seatbelts (driver and passenger)	100
medium suitcase	78	Ski rack	125
small suitcase	74	First aid kit	30
hat suitcase	51	Hazard lights	28
toiletry bag	74	Upgraded heat exchanger	19
leather strap	9	Tinted windows	
Coco floor mats	37	front and side (roadster)	79
Two-tone paint (monochrome)	no charge	front and side (coupé)	56
Two-tone paint (metallic body)	400	front, side, and rear (coupé)	98
Two-tone paint (metallic roof)	170	rear window only (coupé)	19
Ivory steering wheel	no charge	Decorative coupé roof bars necessary	
Leather upholstery	700	for mounting roof racks	85
		Towbar	dealer install

280 SL

Steel unibody with aluminium doors, boot and bonnet

Engine

Name	M 130 (type 130.983)		
Block material	cast iron		
Head material	aluminium		
Cylinders	inline 6		
Cooling	water		
Bore and stroke	86.5 x 78.8mm		
Capacity	2778cc		
Valves	12v sohc		
Compression ratio	9.5:1		
Fuel system	manifold-injection, mechanically controlled, Bosch 6-plunger fuel injection		
Max. power	170bhp @ 5,750rpm (DIN)	180bhp @ 5,700 (SAE)	
Max. torque	177lb/ft @ 4,200rpm (DIN)	193lb/ft @ 4,500rpm (SAE)	
Fuel capacity			

280 SL *CONTINUED*

Transmission

Gearbox Clutch	four-speed manual	four-speed automatic	five-speed manual
Ratios	dry single-plate	fluid coupling	dry single-plate
1st	4.05	3.98	3.92
2nd	2.23	2.52	2.22
3rd	1.4	1.58	1.42
4th	1	1	1
5th	NA	NA	0.85
reverse	3.58	4.15	3.49
Final drive	3.92 (3.69 optional, standard Apr 1970+)	3.92 (3.69 optional, standard Apr 1970+)	4.08

Performance

Top speed	124mph/200km/h	121mph/195km/h	124mph/200km/h
0–62mph (100km/h)	9 secs	9 secs	9 secs

Suspension and Steering

Front	double wishbone, coil springs, torsion bar stabilizer
Rear	single-joint swing axle with compensating spring, coil springs
Steering	recirculating-ball (power optional)
Tyres	185 HR 14
Wheels	steel
Rim width	6 J x 14 HB

Brakes

Type	hydraulic dual-circuit brake system with vacuum booster; disc brakes all four wheels
Size	10.7in front, 11in rear

Dimensions

Track		Overall width	69.3in, 1,760mm
front	58.42in, 1,484mm	Overall height	52in, 1,320mm
rear	58.46in, 1,485mm	Unladen weight	2,998lb, 1,360kg
Wheelbase	94.5in, 2,400mm		
Overall length	168.7in, 4,285mm		

CHAPTER ELEVEN

R107 – THE SUCCESSOR

The R107 was a larger and heavier car than its predecessor, the W113.

Over the years, the 230–280 SLs had quietly proved a point. Just like the tripod star that led every Pagoda SL, the W113 merged the three ideas of the spartan European sports car, soft grand tourer, and road-carving roadster. By not being an extreme example of any of these, the W113 showed it could replace all of them. But in the face of demands for more strength and engine displacement, the baton needed to be passed to a new car that would be built specifically to take forward the SL's reputation of elegance while keeping its power and girth hidden. Over the lifetime of the Pagoda SL

the sports car continued to have its dynamics creep towards the luxury end of the scale. This would be the starting point for the new car, known by code R107.

A New Design

Just as the W113 borrowed many components of Mercedes saloons, the R107 would also pick fruits off the family tree. The front and rear suspension elements were taken from

Idea sketches for the R107, including a targa top.

the W114/W115. That meant a double-wishbone suspension with brake dive support up front., but it was perhaps the rear suspension that saw the most significant improvement. The low-pivot swing axle had grown old in the W113, and the independent rear suspension with semi-trailing arms was a welcome addition to the R107.

The new powerplant was not much of a surprise. Journalists had predicted the addition of a V8 to the W113 years earlier because it made sense to have more power in the sports-car line-up. It had already become clear that the Pagoda SL did not have the right balance for the larger engine, but the R107 was built specifically to accommodate it. The 200bhp (DIN) V8 out of the 280 SE 3.5 would fit nicely under the new bonnet. The suspension was built to carry this kind of weight, and the anti-dive preparations helped ensure there were no problems during heavy braking on the new 350 SL.

3.5-litre M 116 V8 engine in the bay of the 350 SL.

Although the entire world was initially given the 350 SL, not all cars were created equal. America was already receiving 4.5-litre engines instead of the 3.5-litre units, because the emissions regulations sucked out so much power that the extra displacement was needed. On the detuned engines, a lower compression ratio and a milder camshaft choked the cars so much that the jump in capacity – of nearly 30 per cent – did not make much difference in total horsepower (although there was a noticeable rise in torque). This idea of a larger motor would continue on the new SL but, somewhat confusingly, the 4.5-litre cars still carried the 350 SL name.

The body design would help usher in a new corporate face for Mercedes-Benz. Where the W113 had had front fenders that began with a vertical headlight stack that rose above the wheel arches to mimic the pagoda roof, the effect on the new car was quite different. The bonnet lowered to meet a step-down fender line and provided a frame for the flat, rectangular headlights. The front end had large, horizontal features that helped disguise the 70.5in (176.25cm) width of the car. This even carried over on the North American vehicles, which were still stuck with round sealed beams. The turning signal lights and reflectors wrapped around the

Pre-production 350 SL, complete but disguised, undergoing testing at Hockenheimring.

front, eliminating the need for the separate side lights that had been necessary for markets such as the USA and Italy. Where the elegance of the W113 had lain in its uncompli-cated design, the new SL carried many more body lines. But, like a good German, these were attractive in their unclut-tered and well-creased consistency.

Safety was still a buzzword with the 350 SL. The A-pillar was designed to channel water away for better visibility. The tail lights were ribbed, not because they matched the side panels of the car, but because the glass surface was less likely to get dirty. US regulations mandated special bumpers that added another 10in (25cm) to the car's total length. Possibly the greatest safety advantage was the body. The construction of the R107 represented an improvement on the passenger safety cell technology that had gone into the W113. Using computers to design the body shell, Mercedes had produced a structure that was so stiff, it did not even require a roll bar in order to pass the stringent US standards. This improve-ment in safety did mean another gain, though – the R107 weighed 395lb (180kg) more than the final outgoing 280 SL, and the US model was 423lb (192kg) heavier.

The weight gain also reflected another break with tradi-tion on the R107. All SLs before this, including the W194

race car, had a 94.5-in wheelbase. With the addition of 2.4in between the wheels, the 350 SL was a larger car. Also, whereas the W113 had made an attempt to live up to its 'Sports Light' name, with an aluminium boot, bonnet and

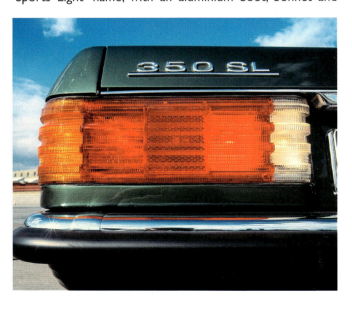

Ribbed taillights repelled dirt.

doors, the R107 was initially produced in a heavier all-steel construction.

The interior of the R107 was much more about personal space than the W113. The modern style dictated that the centre console flowed from the dash panel down past the seats, in the process creating a divide between driver and passenger. The air conditioner was now integrated into the regular ventilation system, so there was no longer any need to save room below the dashboard for this option.

The steering wheel became even safer as the padded centre of the W113 gave way to a new four-spoke unit with a broad, soft safety centrepiece. This wheel would prove to be an icon of Mercedes interior design through the 1980s. It was not exactly the prettiest item for a driver to stare at, but it was the perfect size to accommodate an air bag later in the lifecycle.

The R107 was initially available on the international market with a four-speed manual transmission or an optional three-speed automatic. The new automatic was smoother that the one used in the W113 because it shifted with the use of a hydraulic torque converter. The change did make it much less amenable to being shifted on the move, so the gear selector was eventually changed to a more conventional straight-line set-up.

The extra wheelbase allowed for more room behind the rear seats. As a result, unlike the W113's California Coupé, the new SL could accommodate an optional bench seat and a well to hide the standard soft top. Unfortunately, just like the California Coupé, the space available meant that the rear bench was suitable only for small children. Mercedes had never marketed the SLs as the perfect sports cars for four adults, and, besides, there was now a new car in the line-up for that duty. Half a year after the 350 SL was launched, Mercedes showed off the hard-top 350 SLC at the Paris Motor Show. It resembled the styling of the R107 SL model, but its

The interior of the R107 would increase the safety padding over the W113, including in the steering wheel.

SLCs going through final inspection.

extra 14.2in of wheelbase gave it a much more accommodating back seat. The SLC was developed both out of a fear that the USA would outlaw all convertibles and as a replacement for the 280 SE coupé line-up.

More Engines, Fewer Changes

The confusion in the USA over a car named '350 SL' that had a 4.5-litre motor would not last very long. In 1973, it was renamed the 450 SL. At the same time, Mercedes offered the larger V8 as an option to the rest of the world. The European 450 SL debuted at the Geneva Motor show with the engine producing 225bhp without US emission regulations. Despite Mercedes giving some of its foreign markets the impression that there were two car lines as they made the 230/250 SL switchover, the 450 SL marked the first time there was an actual engine option for the SL.

In Europe, offering the SL line with only 3.5- and 4.5-litre engines was a very risky proposition. For example, in 1971 the UK imported 2.7 times more cars from West

2.8-litre M110 engine of the 280 SL (1974–1985).

Germany with a capacity of 2.8 litres (and under) than cars that reached 3.5 litres. This was especially highlighted following the Yom Kippur War, which created long lines at the petrol pumps at the end of 1973. The Mercedes SL was a luxury item, but there had to be some consideration given to the tax structure and fuel economy that affected everyday ownership. As a result, in August 1974 a 2.8-litre engine was added to the line-up for the return of the 280 SL. The inline six-cylinder would develop 185bhp, but this 15bhp advantage over the previous-generation 280 SL did not outstrip the power/weight ratio of the final W113 cars. Still, it was a welcome addition to the SL line-up, especially since a four-speed manual gearbox was returned, too, so that drivers could opt to get the most out of the smaller engine.

USA GREY IMPORTS

The early 1980s were an interesting time for Mercedes-Benz in the USA. The company had firmly established its image as a manufacturer of luxury vehicles in the US market, and was taking all it could get. With demand far outstripping supply, Mercedes cars such as the SL became a hot item to bring into the country.

Grey-market imports were originally intended for personal use, but a cottage industry sprouted as the mountains of new regulations in the USA began to exclude certain cars. One of the hottest items going was the R107. In fact, that version of the 280 SL was never sold in the US market but, thanks to the grey market, handfuls can still be found today on that side of the Atlantic.

There were even stories of European-spec cars such as the SL coming off the assembly line in Germany and being placed directly on to boats heading across the Atlantic. Once there, the cars would go immediately to a mechanic who would retrofit controls to ensure that the cars conformed to local regulations. Often, the single-piece headlights and smaller bumpers were left in place, and the cars could still be eligible for registration. Compared with contemporary domestic offerings, these cars were lighter, more powerful, and, thanks to European-spec bumpers, much prettier.

Today the grey-market cars are an interesting oddity in America. Much of their design uniqueness has faded away and they should come with a bit of a warning. They comprise many parts that were never intended for the USA, and, with three decades passing since the peak of the grey market Mercedes cars, servicing can be a bit of a problem. Not many of the unique spares are stocked in America, and items such as the non-standard computer system can cause some expensive problems.

US-spec 380 SL, including protruding impact bumpers that made Euro-spec imports popular in the USA.

With the concerns over fuel economy and engine capacity taken care of on the lower end, attention was turned to even larger engines. In 1978 Mercedes developed a 5.0-litre all-alloy V8 that it first tested out on the lower-volume SLC model. The 450 SLC 5.0 developed 240bhp, while the aluminium engine saved 88lb (40kg) over the 4.5-litre iron block off which the new engine design was based. Mercedes put this car on a diet even further by returning the aluminium bonnet and boot-lid of previous SLs and adding aluminium bumpers as well. This shaved another 176lb (80kg) from the speedy machine, and made it the perfect car for Mercedes to take rallying.

The alloy bonnet became part of the entire SL line in 1980. The 5.0-litre V8 became available at this time and replaced the 4.5-litre motor as the top model. Like the SLC, this new 500 SL was given the weight-saving aluminium boot-lid. Any 5.0-litre cars were distinguishable by a discreet front spoiler, a black plastic rear spoiler and uniform grey paint coat under the protective strips at the side.

The mid-pack 350 SL was upgraded to a larger, lighter unit in 1980. A clampdown on European emissions regulations and the ever more stringent US rules had created a need for an all-alloy 3.8-litre to be the middle powerplant in the R107.

350 SL as a coupé, roadster and soft top.

R107 GETS A ROTARY

In the late 1960s, W113 car was given a three-rotor Wankel motor for testing. The compact motor went under the bonnet of the Pagoda, but it took some manoeuvring because the car was not initially designed to accept this new powerplant. This was not true for the R107.

According to Mercedes, the R107's transmission and propshaft tunnel were designed to accommodate the greater installed height of the rotary piston engine with its high central power take-off. In 1971, it took engineers only two months and four days to fit an experimental 277bhp four-rotor motor in a R107 SL. Making the new engine easier to fit also helped expose its faults sooner. 'The priority is to produce an optimum design so as to achieve the most favourable thermodynamic efficiency, i.e. as complete combustion of the fuel as possible,' said Kurt Oblӓnder, a combustion/emissions expert at Mercedes-Benz during this testing era. 'The fact that this did not occur with the Wankel engine, indeed that it could not happen, manifested itself initially in high fuel consumption and later, even more publicly and confirmed officially, in the difficulties in meeting the still quite tame exhaust emission standards for passenger cars due to the high proportion of non-combusted hydrocarbons.'

The inefficiency of the engine led the Mercedes-Benz engineers eventually back to more traditional combustion designs. All of the Wankel experimental SLs were destroyed, but that did not mean there was never a rotary SL on the streets. Dr Felix Wankel asked Mercedes to install one of his namesake engines in his personal R107. Mercedes obliged with a four-rotor unit that made Dr Wankel's car capable of running from 0–125mph in 25.9 seconds and reach a top speed of 149mph (238km/h).

Cross-section of the four-rotor Wankel motor.

It would make 218bhp in Europe and was choked down to 155bhp in America.

The SLC would be dropped in favour of a S-Class-based line of coupés, but the SL continued on into the 1980s with the same body style. By 1985 sales were still strong enough to warrant no more than some minor trim changes and a refreshing of the engine line-up. A 4.2-litre unit replaced the 3.8-litre V8, and the 5.0-litre was revised to produce 245bhp. The 2.8-litre was replaced by a 3.0-litre inline six. This would be the first time a Mercedes would carry the 300 SL badge in over 20 years, but it was a far cry from the original cars, with only 188bhp coming from this motor.

The 500 SL was no longer the top R107 available in some countries. Due to the stringent emissions standards in the USA, Australia and Japan, these markets had the option of ordering a 5.0-litre that was given a longer stroke to a final displacement of 5.6. This motor finally gave these countries an option that came close to their European counterparts because, after it was detuned and the required catalytic converter had been added, the larger V8 put out 230bhp.

Tough Times

Once the R107 had arrived in the 1980s it had already outsold and lived longer than the W113. While its looks certainly helped it move out of Mercedes showrooms, its ability to hold out in the convertible market was a major asset, too. Problems in the USA had become problems for everyone worldwide. The US market was too big to ignore, but no manufacturer could build cars specifically for that market alone. As the list of regulations grew longer and the future of this particular niche became increasingly uncertain future, changes needed to be made at the factory.

Within the first decade of the R107's introduction, the world market for convertibles would shrink. The UK, which was considered the king of the drop-top market, would nearly drop off the map. The uncertainty about its financials, let alone the US regulations, caused conglomerate British Leyland to cancel everything across the board with a cloth hood, from the MGB to the Triumph Stag. Even the Jaguar E-Type, one of the SL's closest competitors aside from price, lost its cloth hood with its successor. The XJS took a page directly from the SL's evolution by becoming more of a grand touring machine, but Jaguar would not even attempt to remove the roof until 1983 (and just barely, with the introduction of the targa-like XJ-SC).

The smaller car manufacturers were certainly not immune. Jensen had tried to build a rival for the SL with its V8 Interceptor convertible, but it failed to make it through 1976. Ferrari opted to stick to more targa-like designs, with cars such as the 308.

The US manufacturers were feeling the pinch, too. Cadillac often competed with Mercedes on price and prestige in the USA, but it would give ground in 1976. One of the hallmarks of the company up until this point had been its offering of a large convertible, but government regulations scared them out of the market.

Mercedes was not the only car company to weather this storm. For example, Volkswagen would keep the Beetle convertible in production into 1980, and then replace it with a Golf unit that included a massive roll bar for safety. At the other end of the spectrum, fear of regulations was hardly going to make Rolls-Royce relinquish the well-heeled end of the convertible market.

As it turned out, of course, the convertible was never outlawed in the USA. Many car manufacturers resumed production of cloth-hooded cars towards the middle of the 1980s, and many of them used the R107 as their prime target. There was plenty of new competition for Mercedes, including Jaguar's proper XJS drop-top and Cadillac's Pininfarina-built Allanté. The R107 had stayed alive in uncertain times, but now, with opposition heating up once again, it was time to step aside. The final R107 was produced in 1989.

Evolution – the SSK, 280 SL, and the 350 SL.

CHAPTER TWELVE

PAGODA RESTORATIONS

A Real Classic

The exact amount of time it takes for a car to be considered a 'classic' is always a matter of debate between enthusiasts, and a matter of opinion among insurance companies and licensing agencies, but for a car to start to draw nostalgic eyes it usually takes a couple of decades. Over a number of years, the bad feelings can melt away and even the homeliest of cars begin to be appreciated. Ford's Edsel was an infamous flop for its few years on the market, but even that lemon-sucker is now a cherished collectable. There are even multiple car clubs that honour the Yugo! So how did a celebrated car like the Pagoda SL fare?

With nearly 50,000 examples produced, seeing a W113 on the road was hardly an event. Schoolboys of the early 1980s were not going to tell tales of seeing a 20-year-old 230 SL

A 250 SL for sale at an enthusiast event. Ironically, this standard coupé (non-California, hardtop not attached) was spotted in Irvine, California.

go by in the same way as they might describe a sighting of a Ferrari, a Rolls-Royce or an Aston Martin from the same era. Even though the SLs were less rare, however, they did not drop in value.

The USA had served as the W113's largest export market, and, during the early 1980s, it was the largest classic-car market in the world. According to pricing data from 1982–1983, as the 230 SL was just beginning to be a classic by age, it was worth around $19,000 in good condition. Even better news was that the younger but very similar 250 and 280 SLs were priced at $15,000–$16,000. Pricing books are a good place to start, but it is not what a car is valued at that determines worth but rather what someone is willing to pay.

Kruse was one of the largest auction houses across the USA in 1982. Its data from nationwide sales showed that, even as the first 230 SLs were entering their twentieth year, buyers were already paying valued classics kind of prices. Cars that were in good condition (very drivable, but not concours quality) were fetching around $12,800. This was nearly double the car's base price, but it was following a period of significant inflation. At about the same time, that kind of money in the US auctions would have purchased a Bentley S3 coupé or two Aston Martin DB5 coupés of a similar condition and model year.

The rarity of the other cars meant that their prices at auction would eventually outdo the Pagoda over the next few decades. By the time the Pagoda was ready to celebrate its 50th anniversary, one Aston Martin DB5 could fetch enough at auction to purchase five 230 SLs in excellent condition. It is not that the market for the W113 has dropped out. The Pagodas have proved to have a long-lasting quality that has allowed them to retain their value, but, because of relatively high production numbers, they do not have the same sort of exclusivity as the Aston Martin. This sustainable value has brought Mercedes back into the business of selling Pagodas.

Restoration Facilities

Mercedes-Benz has created the Classic Centers to capitalize on the demand for its vintage cars. Located in Fellbach, Germany, and Irvine, California, USA, they are restoration facilities that take advantage of Mercedes official parts, service manuals and records to create restorations that make cars nearly factory-fresh. The facilities are set up to handle customer cars as well as projects chosen by the individual Classic Centers. Official company restoration houses of this calibre know the market for classic Mercedes vehicles and

Classic Center trainees restore a Pagoda for a charity project.

only select those that have a market demand. One of the youngest cars that is regularly chosen is the Pagoda SL.

The California facility often has a few Pagoda SLs under restoration. The sunny climate and wealthy clientele base made this a popular sales area for the 230–280 SLs. Now that the Pagoda cars are real classics, the warmth and lack of rain also make the area an ideal hunting ground for restoration candidates.

Restoring a car without having a customer already in line is far from unheard of, but the Classic Center has often taken a unique position. When most cars are restored under speculation, a budget is set and any unforeseen problems could mean cutting other tasks out of the project list. At the Classic Center, the opposite is often true. A car does not leave the Mercedes restoration home shop until the project has met their quality standards. Any problems with a vehicle that went undetected in the initial inspections is often treated as a reason to dive deeper into a restoration and invest more in the car. Because the final product carries

the reputation of Mercedes-Benz, the Classic Center is confident that the time and money that go into a Pagoda will be recovered in the end.

While having a car restored by the manufacturer's official facility is certainly attractive, the Classic Centers are not the only places that can offer Teutonic quality. BRABUS, located outside Essen, about four hours north of where all the W113 cars were built, is a familiar name to those who have looked to get extra luxury and performance out of their Mercedes vehicles. However, for decades they have been keeping a little secret. BRABUS has been in the business of restoring older Mercedes-Benz models since the early 1990s. It was established simply as an on-demand service that was extended to its clients, but that changed with the official opening of BRABUS Classic in 2009. The company still restores cars to client specifications, but now it also actively seeks out candidates for complete restoration. While the company takes on projects such as 300 SL gullwings and 600 Pullmans, there are often a few W113s offered fresh from restoration as well.

W113 rear axle coated during restoration.

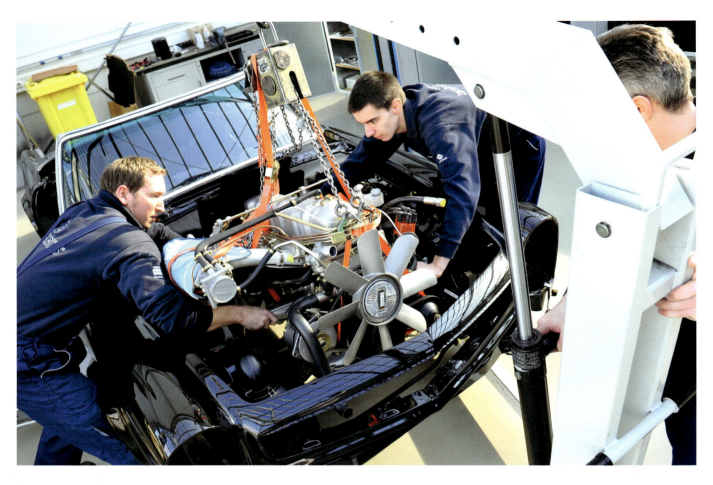

BRABUS installing a motor in a 280 SL.

The majority of the Pagodas were sent to North America and the car has become a speciality on that continent. German-born Gernold Nisius has owned SL-Tech in Arundel, Maine, for over two decades. Nisius is in a unique position, having been apprenticed to his hometown Mercedes-Benz shop outside Ramstein in the early 1970s, just as the W113 had finished its production run. Due to the Pagoda's high price and his relatively rural surroundings, each W113 that he spotted left a lasting impression on the young man. 'When I was a kid that was *the* car', he remembers. Later, he would gain experience servicing the handful of 230/250/280 SLs that were in his area.

After he mastered his craft, Nisius moved to the USA, where the abundance of W113s allowed him to make it his only focus. His business is not just about restoration; he also stocks as many spares as he can get to fill his store room. While Mercedes is one of the best car companies for offering official parts decades after the car is gone, they cannot pro-

vide everything. Nisius pays special attention to items such as minor interior trim pieces that will never be reproduced, and will make a car look somewhat awkward if they are missing.

Nisius also sees a growing problem for right-hand-drive W113s. Countries such as Australia, Japan and Britain were not top export destinations for Mercedes-Benz during the era of the Pagoda. This means that unique right-hand drive pieces, ranging from the dashboard to the glovebox lid to the firewall, are already in short supply, and have become coveted components.

While each restoration has its own set of needs, Nisius does see a few repeated problems. For example, any car that has not had a recent restoration often needs its heater serviced. Not every car from the 1960s had a useful heater, and so Nisius often sees people who do not realize that they have a problem until he tells them: 'You should actually see your hair going when it's blowing.' This hardly seems extraordinary

A restoration comes down to details. Note the marking line just above the tape on the headlight surround that was used to correctly align the lights and is often missing if a W113 has been hastily repainted.

BELOW: **A before and after shot of a nearly completed restoration at Nisius's shop.**

today, but in an era when car heaters had varying degrees of usefulness, this was one reason why the W113 was a premium vehicle. With an effective heater, open-top motoring could still be comfortable even on an autumn day. Often, owners miss out on this feature and settle for a system that rivals the infamous draft of hot air that came in the Volkswagen Beetle.

It is not just in the way in which the components function that Nisius sees the quality in these cars. To him, the Pagoda represents the pinnacle of German craftsmanship. The car may look simple by modern standards, but Nisius knows that appearances can be deceiving. 'It's always built to outlast us or more', is how he describes the Mercedes engineering approach.

It may seem ironic that a man who takes apart these cars for a living cherishes the idea of all the extra screws and welds that make his job harder. But, in the end, it is the lasting quality that has helped to build the legacy of this car.

The Best Car to Restore?

Choosing between the three versions of the W113 can be a bit daunting. One of the more general rules to follow comes from Mercedes-Benz Classics: simply find the car in the best condition. There are people who are set on a specific model or who have an emotional connection to a specific car, but, for those who just want a Pagoda, this is good advice. After all, each car has its own set of merits.

The 230 SL is considered to be the most spirited of the bunch. The 250 SL is by far the rarest and offers more power and often more safety features than the 230 SL. The 280 SL has the largest motor of the group. As far as coupé, roadster or convertible is concerned, the same rules of the cars being interchangeable when new still apply today. There are Mercedes and aftermarket parts as well as spares that can help to turn almost any solid Pagoda into each person's ideal classic.

It is good to remember that the four-passenger California Coupé is the rarest W113 body style available, and it is not compatible with the other versions of the Pagoda cars. This leaves owners with a removable hard top with no conventional option for fitting a canvas hood (although there are some plans to add a folding cloth hood that was not issued by Mercedes-Benz). Any retrofit to a California Coupé is more for a skilled home mechanic and is still rare on the market. This leaves the car with a limited functionality that currently means that it often enters the market at a lower price than other comparable W113s. A buyer should not pay extra to any seller advertising the uniqueness of his California Coupé.

When it comes to the mechanical components to differentiate the various W113 models, the debate is generally futile. All of the suspension components that differed between the 230, 250 and 280 SLs when they left the factory should no longer matter. One of the cornerstones of Mercedes' reputation for reliability is the fact that they have spares available for long after a car has left production. The W113 had multiple versions of front springs, rear springs, shock absorbers and anti-roll bars, but it would be almost impossible for Mercedes-Benz to keep every part for every car they ever made. Instead, its technical manuals are updated for the latest parts available. This means that, as the sealed drivetrain components became standard on the 280 SL, they soon also became the stock replacement parts for the 230 and 250 SLs.

This upgrade seems to be somewhat unavoidable. For example, anyone buying a well-travelled pre-1968 W113 should find that many of its main suspension parts should have been changed during its decades on the road. Someone restoring a barn-find 230 SL might find that the car comes with some of its original suspension parts, but any components ordered from Mercedes will include the latest version

280 SL restored by BRABUS, including Fuchs wheels.

of the sealed units updated to the specs of the 280 SL. This is a positive point because, in the end, the Pagoda SLs are very drivable classics that can be on the road for decades, with little fear of service problems. The narrowing of differences between the models means there is a larger pool of people who need the same part, which makes it viable for Mercedes-Benz and the aftermarket to continue carrying spare components.

Just because something is available does not necessarily mean it is discounted. A car that is built well initially will have a serious impact on the wallet when going into restoration – it takes more time and money to replace quality. Usability and durability are part of the W113's allure to collectors and, although a 230/250/280 SL might require less work than some of its other European counterparts, the costs can often add up to the same, or more. In addition, parts sharing does not include unique elements such as body panels and some smaller components, so it is good to consult a Mercedes specialist and/or Pagoda car clubs first to find out which W113 pieces might be in short supply.

The final piece in the collection puzzle is how original an enthusiast wants his or her Pagoda to be. It is now up to the individual collector where to draw the line between originality and added comforts. One of the 230 SL's most significant differences is its rear drum brakes, but it is quite feasible to retrofit rear discs (a few even escaped the factory with four discs as original equipment towards the end of the 230 SL run). Also, if there is a desire for more power, modern performance components can squeeze more out of any of the three motors available in the W113.

A STANDOUT AMONG CLASSICS

The W113 cars are far from exclusive to Mercedes-specialist shops. Jason Wenig owns the Creative Workshop in Dania Beach, Florida. Their domain runs to whatever is unique, which has led to everything from winning awards at the Pebble Beach Concours d'Elégance to recrafting prototypes back to their show car days. So, while he has scoured the world with clients hunting down bespoke machines, Wenig has also found that a more mass-produced car like the 230/250/280 SL has become a growing request on his clients' lists:

Over the years, we have restored, serviced, repaired and maintained many Pagoda SLs. It seems many of my clients – or perhaps classic car enthusiasts in general – are attracted to this car. Taking a step back and thinking about it for a moment, it is obvious why. First and foremost, I would consider them unisex rides. A woman is as equally comfortable and looking good behind the wheel as a man. So even the hardcore car-collecting men who fit the stereotype of having their abundance of toys can purchase a 280 SL for their wife and allow them to participate in the hobby with them. I don't feel too surprised when the men end up driving it as much as the spouse. After all, the Pagoda styling is somewhat neutral in that the car is sort of like a classic tuxedo or a woman's 'little black dress'... it looks good on everybody.

Their level of sophistication also makes them much simpler to enjoy. Vintage European autos often mean setting a choke, pumping a carburettor, or any other combination of arcane things we must do to get a 45-plus-year-old piece of machinery to come to life. A person who might not be comfortable with these rituals can simply put the key in a 230 SL, start it, and drive. Compared to its Italian and British counterparts, I consider the Mercedes is sort of like 'classic car lite'. You get most of the benefits of a true classic car with few of the typical bugaboos.

The Pagoda is also perhaps a perfect blend between price/value/cost. They are expensive enough to be 'exclusive' but not nearly costly enough to come across snobbish or snooty. Parts are readily available. Camaraderie comes from a very strong support group to help with most questions and to participate in gatherings, if that is your thing. Also, the car's appreciation has kept up nicely with the appreciation of the classic-car market. This adds to a tone of 'smartness' to your choice in car, which only helps to perpetuate its value. Looks good, performs well, presents the right image, is 'a sound investment', etc. – it is no wonder so many people really like this car.

A STANDOUT AMONG CLASSICS *CONTINUED*

Restored motor freshly installed in a 280 SL at The Creative Workshop.

On the negative side, however, there are some genuine concerns. When I've met with clients to discuss a W113 project, I sometimes have to give them a dose of reality that comes with their dream car. First on the list is that I have to remind them that the Pagodas are thoroughly a Mercedes – everything is over-engineered. It can sound like a fortunate 'problem' to have but not when you see the invoice. Something that could be accomplished for $5 and one screw has been 'MB'd', and it will cost $25 and has six screws. Along the same lines, most wear-out/replacement parts are available to purchase reproduction or brand-new from Benz Classic, but the price tag of parts is very high. This, like the 190 SL, is certainly a contributing factor to the rise in cost of these vehicles. Anyone who knows about them, knows how expensive it is for upkeep, and now that is also usually reflected/factored into the acquisition cost.

Perhaps the most dramatic (negative) personality trait of this car is the raw nature of the drive. History remembers the car as a sophisticated roadster, but that was in an era when disc brakes were a luxury item. It has one of the best daily driver appeals of any 40-plus-year-old sports car out there, but the 230/250/280 SLs still cannot escape their age. The suspension is a bit stiff and hard for modern standards, but it is the engine that really takes some time for today's new owners to understand.

Be prepared for a high-revving, loud driving experience. You get used to it, but the first 100 miles, you will be constantly looking for another gear (I have seen more prototype Maseratis pass through my shop than five-speed ZF Pagodas). This car/engine was designed to cruise in the 2,800–3,500rpm range and, on acceleration, you can hear and feel the six-cylinder engine really stretching out to pull the car. The exhaust note is sporty, but it is far from the religious experience of a V12 Ferrari. While this sustained high range can give the initial impression that something needs to be tuned or fixed, it really is just this car's comfort zone. This SL can and will perform at these high revs all day and all night. A bit odd for those used to the more tame nature of today's Mercedes-Benzs, but as long as you are prepared/expecting it, you'll be fine.

These kind of negative points are often corrected with a bit of driver retraining, which only helps this car's folklore grow. Just as classic Porsche 911 drivers wear their knowledge of oversteer as a badge of honour, Pagoda SL drivers gain an instinct for running higher rpms.

In the end, I've never had a client who has found the negatives of a 230/250/280 SL to be a deal breaker. Restoring them has often just been an 'eyes open' experience where the pluses strongly outweigh the minuses.

(Jason Wenig)

Jason Wenig with a Motto-bodied MG restored by his shop.

CHAPTER THIRTEEN

TIMELESS STYLE

While Sir Stirling Moss is one of the best endorsements for a precision vehicle, he was just one of the car's celebrity owners. He was not even the only racer to enjoy a Pagoda off the track. Mercedes drivers Juan-Manuel Fangio, Jack Brabham and David Coulthard have all been seen behind the wheel of a W113.

Before John Lennon became known as the owner of a psychedelic Rolls-Royce Phantom V, he ordered a blue on

grey 230 SL, in 1965. Other singing idols, from 1950s teen heart-throb Ricky Nelson to soul singer Tina Turner, were also attracted to these SLs. Elvis Presley might have been famous for giving away Cadillacs to friends and family, but it is his wife Priscilla's white 280 SL that gets a feature spot in the motor museum next to his former Graceland home.

When rocket pioneer Wernher von Braun was working at NASA, he was also a friend of Mercedes in the USA,

Juan-Manuel Fangio and his W113.

JOHN LENNON'S PAGODA

John Lennon's 230 SL at the Sarasota Classic Car Museum.

In early 1965, the Beatles released *Ticket to Ride*, and John Lennon finally got his driving licence at the age of 25. His first car would be a 1965 Ferrari 330 GT 2+2 Berlinetta, but it was not the only vehicle he purchased that year. By the end of that summer he had also become the owner of a Pagoda.

The Beatles began their second US tour on 15 August 1965 in New York, with a record-setting concert at Shea Stadium. Three days before that, a 1965 Mercedes 230 SL had been registered to a John Winston Lennon. The automatic transmission roadster may have been distinctly German, but the colour scheme was very British. The hue of the grey interior took on the properties of some of the deep blue body, creating a dark-on-light blue impression that would not be out of place on a Bentley.

Although Lennon sold his first Ferrari in October 1967, he held on to his Pagoda for nearly a year longer. The right-hand drive 230 SL was sold to its second owner in November 1968 and the car would pass through a series of hands in the UK before being sent to California in 1995.

Lennon's Pagoda SL is now housed in the Sarasota Classic Car Museum in Florida. The museum has a treasure trove of other Beetles cars, including a Paul McCartney Mini and psychedelic Bentley S1 (not unlike Lennon's more famous Rolls-Royce Phantom V). The 230 SL is parked on display next to Lennon's 1979 Mercedes-Benz 300TD Estate, rather like unfortunate bookends representing the beginning and end of his driving era.

There is a distinct benefit to having this 230 SL in Florida, besides the opportunity it presents for a sunny day out. The car is registered in that state and, when it is not on display with a replica of Lennon's original GGP 196C number plate, it carries a local tag. Florida drivers have the opportunity to buy a special number plate from the state, with the extra fees going towards fighting hunger across the state. In honour of Lennon's song and philosophy, the number plate has the word 'Imagine' on top, with the authorized use of his self-portrait in the middle.

JOHN LENNON'S PAGODA *CONTINUED*

Florida 'Imagine' number plate with proceeds to help fight hunger.

Interior, Lennon's Pagoda.

and joined the Mercedes-Benz North America supervisory board in 1965. This association helped launch the Mercedes for Astronauts initiative. At the time, most of America's highest-flying heroes were in Corvettes because of an ambitious local General Motors dealer, but that did not stop some from taking advantage of the Mercedes programme. In fact, the first American in space, John Glenn, was another famous figure who owned a Pagoda.

Cars as Stars

Movie stars such as John Travolta, Peter Ustinov and Charlton Heston were fond of the W113 off the screen, but that is only half of the story. The 230–280 SLs has played a distinctive role in films and on television.

In the automotive world an icon is a star that shines so bright during its lifetime that it remains a long-standing symbol of its era. In the 1960s, film was beginning to turn the car into the star. The Mini achieved its icon status being driven around Italy by Michael Caine and friends for *The Italian Job*, while Dustin Hoffman did the same for his Alfa Romeo, sprinting up and down the California coast in *The Graduate*. But there was another kind of icon on screen that established its notoriety by helping tell the character's story just by being behind the wheel. The Pagoda SL has played this role for over 50 years.

The 1967 film *Two for the Road* looks back at a couple spending their youth getting across France by hitching rides or driving a well-worn MG. At the beginning, Audrey Hepburn and Albert Finney are depicted in modern times, as beautiful and wealthy people who are well established in life. What other car would they take with them on a road trip but a 230 SL?

Characters in movies and television are grounded by the props they use. While having a character behind the wheel of a Pagoda SL might not seem like much, set designers and prop masters will often use a certain car to make that character believable. It has worked in all sorts of ways, from highlighting an antagonist's wild jealousy in Disney's *That Darn Cat* (1965), by having him trade in his sensible saloon for a two-seat sports car, to giving Sharon Tate's bumbling international spy persona a bit of legitimacy in Dean Martin's *The Wrecking Crew* (1968).

Staying in the Public Eye

There was no decade in which this car was out of fashion. When the rich kid from the privileged side of town was not on his bicycle in 1979's *Breaking Away*, he drove a W113. Julie Andrews tried to wrangle in her midlife-crisis boyfriend while speeding around the Hollywood hills in her 280 SL as one of the few sensible minds in Blake Edward's *10*.

Waiting for some movie magic – 280 SL features at a classic car dealearship in Beverly Hills, California.

Possibly one of the best uses of the Pagoda's staying power was in *The Long Good Friday*. When the film was first released, in late 1980, the 280 SL used was about a decade old. Bob Hoskins' patriotic Harold Shand had a younger Rolls-Royce and a nearly-new Jaguar XJ6. His right-hand man was better educated, with an upper-class sensibility. The film begins during a long-standing peace in the London underworld, and the young Jeff does not need to drive a gangster's car. An Alfa Romeo would have made him a playboy; a Jaguar XJS would be too flash; and a *new* Mercedes would just be showing up his boss. Jeff's Pagoda SL told the audience this character's background without saying a word. He was privileged, ambitious and style-conscious, and his image was established the moment he arrived at Shand's yacht in his 280 SL.

Another interesting example was the use of the car in the film *Intersection*, a remake of the French film *Les Choses de la Vie*. It was far from the most popular film of 1994, but it did give Richard Gere a chance to demonstrate many of the Pagoda SL's best attributes. He plays a wealthy architect who owns a 280 SL that is over two decades old. It is seen as a modern classic and is an extension of his style. The main catalyst for the plot is a horrific car accident that involves three vehicles, including a lorry. While movie magic re-creates a 75mph accident, the W113 takes multiple collisions and rolls down a hill, yet the passenger cell remains in fairly good condition.

Now that the Pagoda SL has been around for over half a century, it is used as a signpost on film to remind audiences of the era from which it came. This started as early as 1975, in the movie *Shampoo*, which came out only a few years after the W113 had been retired. By using the car, Warren Beatty's character was firmly located in 1968. In *The Last King of Scotland* (2006), Forest Whitaker as Idi Amin uses one of the last series of 280 SLs to keep his fictitious doctor (James McAvoy) under his spell as he consolidates power. A W113 is used to bring a little light into the life of an MI6 agent in Istanbul for the 2011 film adaptation of John le Carré's *Tinker Tailor Soldier Spy*.

The television series *Mad Men* used a W113 as the car that represented a getaway to 1962 California. This was completely wrong, since the first 230 SLs were not produced until the summer of 1963 and only arrived in the USA in the autumn, nearly a year *after* the time of the show's storyline. Still, that quick flash of the car at a valet stand was effective in creating a rich flavour of the time.

A Timeless Fashion Icon

The elegant appearance of the Pagoda SL also makes it an accessory in the world of fashion. Brooks Brothers, Harper's Bazaar and J. Crew have all used the Pagoda SL in their advertising.

Kevin Caputo's 230 SL being prepared for a catalogue shoot for Ralph Lauren.

One of the more interesting advertisements in recent years from the fashion industry has been for Juicy Couture. It features a model sitting on the boot-lid of a white 280 SL that is parked on a nearly empty southern California street. This would be almost unremarkable, were it not for the fact that the only other car on the street is a white R107. Since this is not an ad for cars, the photographer's focal point is not on this little mystery of the W113 replacement parked slightly out of focus. Is the implication that, since the model knows fashion, she also knows that she should choose to sit on the W113 instead of its successor?

The individual cars chosen for these campaigns are not necessarily props owned by studios. Kevin Caputo is one private owner who knows this first-hand. He has an interesting 230 SL that has played its part in some fashionable advertisements. It was built in November 1966 and sold as a US-spec 1967 model, at the same time as the first 250 SLs were lurking on the same assembly line at Sindelfingen. The white on black car would have four decades of owners before it was purchased by Kevin Caputo in 2005.

Within his first year of ownership Kevin answered a posting on the sl113.org enthusiast website, looking for a Pagoda to use in a photo shoot near his home in Miami, Florida. Ralph Lauren wanted to portray a modern man with a sense of classical style, and a Coral Gables mansion and the Pagoda car on their catalogue cover were perfect for conveying that message.

Although his car is a star, Kevin has never thought about cashing in his 230 SL. The year and the colour remind him of his first car (a Chevrolet), and the tri-star badge fulfilled a promise to return to a classic Mercedes after he sold his 1973 280C a couple of decades earlier to pay for his wedding. While having it in a photo shoot was fun, Kevin's passion for his Pagoda runs deeper.

The W113 was the subject of many misunderstandings over the years. There were other sports cars available on the market that cost less and were quicker, yet the Pagoda SL was a sales success. Of course, much of its appeal lay in the fact that it was a well-balanced driver's car, but there was another factor at play that was less tangible but immediately felt: elegance. Possibly one of the best ways the W113 proves its timeless style is in the way that the car was immediately fashionable when it left the factory – and remains chic today.

The final results of the shoot.

Thu Stubbs and her beloved 280 SL. JIM GUZEL/APHRODITE PHOTOGRAPHY

Fashion for a Lifetime

Thu Stubbs fell in love with Pagodas at an early age. Her father was an American army officer who was stationed in what was at the time West Germany. On a daddy-daughter walk through Frankfurt one day, the pre-teen saw a bright flash in the road. A silver W113 had caught her eye like nothing else before. As Stubbs questioned her father, who was an enthusiast, he told her some of the information about the car. Pagodas were already on their way to becoming classics, so her father suggested that any W113 would be bought with her own money and not as the next family car.

Stubbs eventually returned to the USA, passed her driving test and attended college, but she never forgot about the Pagoda. As new cars began to let function and regulations dictate their style, the W113 became more desirable. 'It was the last SL with romantic curves', she said.

During her education, Stubbs signed up for the Reserve Officer Training Corps (ROTC) and was given an army commission on graduation. She asked to be assigned to West Germany. This was where she grew up, and her knowledge of the German and French languages would be put to good use. But there was another reason in the back of her mind. It was US Army policy to ship back personal vehicles on an officer's return to the USA, so Stubbs knew that this assignment could help her to acquire the dream car from her youth.

In 1986, while at the base store for the Patch Barracks in Stuttgart, Stubbs saw a bulletin board ad for a 1968 Mercedes 280 SL. She quickly took down the number and headed home. When she phoned about the car for sale, the owner had no idea what she was taking about. He did have a silver 280 SL with a four-speed manual gearbox, but he had never posted an advertisement and had no intention of

Thu was quite happy that she was able to keep elements like the European-spec headlights when she imported the car to the USA. JIM GUZEL/ APHRODITE PHOTOGRAPHY

BELOW RIGHT: **This means more than just chrome and metal to Thu.** JIM GUZEL/APHRODITE PHOTOGRAPHY

selling it. Stubbs and the man eventually figured out that it was the owner's wife who had placed the ad. She had told her husband that he could only have one 'toy', and a recent boat purchase meant that the Pagoda had to go. While the man was adamant that it was still *his* car, he did invite Stubbs to come and see it.

They met at a garage on the outskirts of Stuttgart. The man lifted the door, and Stubbs immediately fell in lust. 'It was the car I saw as a little girl', she remembered after first laying eyes on the silver on black 280 SL convertible.

The owner proudly gave Stubbs a tour of his Pagoda. He talked about every detail, from the sheepskin seat covers for the cold winters, to only being able to afford a half respray because of the level of quality he demanded. The car looked perfect, and Stubbs knew that she had found a kindred spirit. As is often the case in these situations, Stubbs was convinced that this was going to be her car but not quite yet. She gave her contact details to the owner with a plea to call her first when he was ready to part with his Pagoda. To her surprise, he called back within a few weeks. He was only prepared to give up his 280 SL if it went to a good home like his. The car was sold with the stipulation that the new owner would

keep it and drive it, and not just sell it for a profit. She had no problem with that.

Thu Stubbs rented a garage and drove her SL in Germany for a few years. When she was discharged from the Army, it was shipped to Baltimore, Maryland. Despite all the changes that a new 280 SL needed to be certified in the USA, Stubbs had very little trouble getting the Euro-spec car back to her home country. She got to keep the Bosch Lichteinheits, kilometre speedometer, and the engine, which was not choked by US emission standards. One of the most problematic items was a lighting switch that was not labelled (regulations required all operations to be marked), but that was fairly easily remedied with a home-made tag. The car even became a motivator for her to find a new home as soon as possible, so that it could return to being garage kept.

Although this cherished 280 SL has been getting regular use for many decades, it is as tidy as the day it was picked it up in Germany, preserved with regular maintenance. Stubbs cannot recall exactly how many miles she has added to its tally, because to her that has never been a priority. Her Pagoda has pride of place in her garage, and the only factor that dictates her annual distances is how many fair-weather days allow her to take the top down and enjoy it.

Thu Stubbs often shares her story at car shows and she knows how to attract the right attention. In her 1960s-era dresses, she looks as fashionable as her car when they go out for a drive together. While this is all good fun, the style of her Pagoda is at the heart of her enduring zeal for the vehicle. 'The car is made of unbroken lines', she explains. 'It's like a woman's stiletto high heels.'

CHAPTER FOURTEEN

GOING FORWARD

The W113 may have not been the first SL, but it set the tone to move forwards. Today, the spirit of the 300 SL has been reborn in supercars such as the Mercedes SLR and the SLS AMG. The 190 SL's open-top thrills on a more obtainable budget live on in the SLK. It was the introduction of the 230 SL that set the path for the modern Mercedes-Benz SL-Class.

Since the era of the W113, the successors have grown in size, technology and power. Where the 230 SL would top out at 124mph, the latest cars are electronically limited to stay under 200mph. But even as these road cars achieve feats once thought exclusive to race cars, they have not lost the ability to be sporting without being intimidating. It is an important distinction, which allows an SL to sold on prestige as much as precision. Cars from performance marques such as Porsche and Ferrari have adapted to this personality over the last half-century, but the Mercedes W113 planted the SL's roots in this concept.

Part of the reason why the SL-Class has earned its reputation for being so inviting is its commitment for safety. The W113 was born just as the protection of passengers from harm became a cornerstone of Mercedes technical development. The 230 SL was the first sports car with a safety body and since then Mercedes has made sure that with speed comes security.

A car is made from bits of metal, plastic and rubber – a bunch of emotionless materials that, when assembled correctly, can create a feeling. In the case of the W113, that feeling is desire. It is a car that has good lines that are not too trendy nor too old-fashioned. It has a classical beauty that has been part of the styling direction of its successors. The Pagoda's legacy is its grace.

The prestige in owning a Pagoda and its successors is not masculine or feminine. Instead, ownership is more of a declaration of knowing that there is luxury in precision.

The SL has grown over time, but the first SLK returned to the magic 94.5in (2400mm) wheelbase.

The W113 picked up the SL baton and proved itself worthy by combining Mercedes-Benz's reputation for sporting cars, well-built reliable machines and premium image. While its successors grew in size, price and available power, the Pagoda's fingerprints can still be seen today.

INDEX